Training Through Dialogue

Training Through Dialogue

Promoting Effective Learning and Change with Adults

Jane Vella

Jossey-Bass Publishers • San Francisco

Substantial discounts on bulk quantities of Jossey-Bass books are available to corporations, professional associations, and other organizations. For details and discount information, contact the special sales department at Jossey-Bass Inc., Publishers.

(415) 433–1740; Fax (800) 605–2665.

For sales outside the United States, please contact your local Simon & Schuster International Office.

Excerpts from Paulo Freire, *Pedagogy of the Oppressed* (rev. 1993) reprinted by permission of the Continuum Publishing Company.

Quote from *Death of a Salesman* by Arthur Miller copyright 1949, renewed © 1977 by Arthur Miller. Used by permission of Viking Penguin, a division of Penguin Books USA Inc.

 Manufactured in the United States of America on Lyons Falls Pathfinder Tradebook. This paper is acid-free and 100 percent totally chlorine-free.

Library of Congress Cataloging-in-Publication Data

Vella, Jane Kathryn, date.
    Training through dialogue: promoting effective learning and
change with adults / Jane Vella. — 1st ed.
        p.   cm. — (The Jossey-Bass higher and adult education series)
    Includes bibliographical references and index.
    ISBN 0-7879-0135-0
    1. Adult education teachers—Training of. 2. Adult learning.
3. Popular education. I. Title. II. Series.
LC5225.T4V45 1995
370' .71—dc20   95-19860

FIRST EDITION
HB Printing   10 9 8 7 6 5 4 3 2 1

The Jossey-Bass Higher and Adult Education Series

Consulting Editor
Adult and Continuing Education

Alan B. Knox
University of Wisconsin, Madison

Contents

Preface

The concept of popular education has grown out of the seminal work of Brazilian educator Paulo Freire (1970, 1993) and is reflected in the work of adult educators from the United States such as Stephen Brookfield, Malcolm Knowles, Alan Knox, Donald Oliver, Donald Schön, and Ira Schor, who recognize that traditional schoolroom teaching is not usually a healthy approach to instructing adults who come to the classroom knowing what they want and need to learn. What is known in Latin America as "educación popular" is closely related to what Knowles calls "andragogy," and to what others call learner-centered education or "action learning."

This book offers a model of popular education characterized by learners' participation in naming content via needs assessment, mutual respect, dialogue between learner and teacher and among learners, achievement-based learning objectives, small-group work to engage learners and to provide safety, visual support and psycho-motor involvement, accountability of the teacher to do what he or she proposes, student participation in the evaluation of program results, a listening attitude on the part of teachers and resource people, and learning by doing.

Most educators recognize that they teach in the same way as they were taught. Unless their training provides them with a new experience of education, as teachers they will revert to their known framework, their familiar model. How can graduate students in adult education, public school adult educators who teach adults in English as a Second Language (ESL), Adult Basic Education (ABE), and General Education Diploma (GED) classrooms, trainers in industry and government, agricultural extension agents, and health educators be given such a compelling experience of popular education that they are moved to compare this model with what they have known all their lives? Can teachers of adults be taught in such an accountable and participative manner that they learn to critically examine the philosophical assumptions, principles, and practices both of the old, familiar model and of this new approach? This book aims to respond to these tough questions.

What This Book Has to Offer

Like my previous book, *Learning to Listen, Learning to Teach* (1994), which showed how adult education can be structured around adult learners' needs, this book offers examples from a variety of settings of how to prepare trainers and educators to use the popular education approach. In the earlier book, I named a dozen principles of adult learning that I had discovered to be operative in the popular-education approach: (1) needs assessment; (2) safety; (3) a sound relationship between teacher and adult student; (4) sequence and reinforcement of content; (5) praxis—that is, action with reflection; (6) learners as subjects of their own learning; (7) the use of ideas, feelings, and actions in learning; (8) immediacy; (9) a new role for the teacher; (10) teamwork; (11) engagement; and (12) accountability. In this book, I will go further and examine additional principles and practices that are necessary for adult educators.

The book is not a history of popular education in the United States or Latin America. It is also not definitive of any but my own empirically based theory. If my position differs from that of Paulo Freire or other sages in adult education, I celebrate that difference and stand on my own epistemological ground, knowing what my own experience has proven to me and acknowledging that on whatever ground I stand I am also always standing on the shoulders of my own teachers. These teachers have emphasized those elements that assure accountable adult learning: honoring the autonomy of learners, showing them respect, listening to them, engaging them actively in the learning process, and inviting critical thinking. These elements lend themselves naturally to community education efforts. I am proposing in this book, however, that many of the principles and practices of popular education apply to all educational efforts with adults. I am deeply concerned about the danger adult learners face when they are taught by people who do *not* honor these basic principles of adult learning.

Imagine, for example, software networking consultants trained in the popular education approach, preparing their presentation to representatives of local business groups on the potential of the network software they sell. Instead of simply deciding what they are going to cover in their presentation and preparing the necessary overheads and handouts, they begin their preparation by doing a needs assessment by telephone with those registered for the training. During the session, they create maximum safety by using small groups throughout the process, testing handouts for valid sequence and adequate reinforcement, inviting and affirming the questions of learners, asking them to set up three or four possible situations within the presentation to ensure that they know how to use the software. Imagine these consultants calling a sample of participants a few weeks after the presentation to inquire how well they are doing with their new software and to ask about any problems they may be facing in using it. This is adult education with a respectful eye on the learner, an example of what this book refers to as popular education. It involves relentless dialogue. Throughout this book I will demonstrate one way of teaching men and women to use this approach.

The dialogue between us—you, dear reader, and me—will be a function of your critical reading of this process of training-the-trainer as it unfolds in six different settings in six chapters. In each chapter there will be sections inviting your criticism, called "Your

Turn." I expect that readers of this book will be men and women who already have strong ideas about adult learning and are ready to offer new criticism of the popular education approach.

Who Will Find This Book Useful?

I trust that this book will be read and used by men and women who either design, implement, or manage adult education and training in industry, government, churches, clinics and health maintenance organizations, nonprofit organizations, community-based organizations, international development agencies, the Peace Corps, and Americorps. Adult educators dealing with new skills and concepts can use this book both to learn how popular education approaches can enhance their work and to learn how to train others to use this approach. Technical trainers, those who teach men and women to teach others basic skills in industry, who wish to give trainers a new model, would do well to read this book. I hope that the book will reach public school teachers working in ABE and GED classrooms and those who do staff development programs with peers. In addition, I have tried to make this book appealing to graduate students in adult education and their professors so that they will examine the model of popular education critically and thus learn from it to design their own personal set of principles and practices. I also want this book to send readers to the writings of the seminal thinkers behind it: Paulo Freire, Kurt Lewin, Malcolm Knowles, and Alan Knox.

The fact that undergraduate and graduate students are adults is often underestimated. I would be delighted if this book and its predecessor were also useful to those who offer suggestions for improved teaching to professors in colleges and universities. In my experience, the principles and practices of popular education have proven applicable with adults in any setting.

I would be very pleased to hear that men and women who design training programs for educators in health care, education for literacy, community organizing, family planning, and the like were

able to use these principles and practices to design successful training programs. The six examples I provide include the training of
literacy trainers, health educators, small-business developers, community educators dealing with AIDS, professionals training on the
issue of substance abuse, and trainers in various not-for-profit groups.
I hope this diversity provides a useful fit for all who are searching for
a meaningful, accountable, respectful way to teach adults.

Overview of the Contents

The book is organized into three parts. Part One consists of two
chapters. In Chapter One I present the epistemology, or theory of
knowledge, behind popular education, and the assumptions I see
underlying it. In Chapter Two I describe a generic popular education training course.

Part Two consists of six chapters (Chapters Three through
Eight) offering evidence of the effectiveness of the principles and
practices that bear out the hypothesis presented in Part One. Each
chapter presents the story of a particular train-the-trainers program:
one in Chile with community health educators; one in rural
Arkansas with small business developers and trainers in community banking; one in New England with trainers from a number of
diverse nonprofit organizations; one in Syracuse, New York, with
literacy professionals; one in a veterans hospital in the southern
United States with professionals who teach patients about substance abuse; and one in Haiti with community educators who
form a coalition against the spread of AIDS. The development of
each program is described—how it was conceived, designed, and
checked against the expectations and needs of participants; highlights are given of each program; and, finally, something of the
process by which the effects of each program were or are evaluated
is presented, including indicators of changed behavior in individuals who took part in the particular program. Each chapter
includes a summary section that invites the reader's critique and
suggestions.

The three chapters in Part Three demonstrate how the conceptual framework is both always the same and always changing to meet a new context. Chapter Nine demonstrates how the principles and practices can be put to work in designing a train-the-trainers program for a difficult situation—specifically, an urban police department. Chapter Ten shows some options for follow-up and support of newly trained trainers. Chapter Eleven looks at evaluation. A glossary of terms that are used throughout the book is included at the end of the chapters.

Throughout the book I have tried to use the principles I am endeavoring to teach, so that the reading is itself an experience of the popular education method. An adult educator who read my first book said wistfully, "I wished it would go right from my head to my hands!" My approach in this book is to facilitate that movement, from head to hands, I hope by way of the heart. That is why the book contains numerous anecdotes and lots of philosophy in between the lines of the technical program.

To be consistent with the principles of popular education, I have taken Freire's problem-posing approach, which holds that learning is most effective and transformative as dialogue. Each of the six stories in Part Two is a codification or representation of the problems most educators encounter in setting out to design a train-the-trainers program. As you "decodify" each situation by your critique and analysis, learning can take place.

Research has shown that skills are not learned only by reading a book. Many educators who read *Learning to Listen, Learning to Teach* came later to training workshops and said, "Now I understand what you were trying to say in your book!" This book is only a prelude to what can be learned in an actual train-the-trainers program that clearly endeavors to demonstrate and teach cognitive, affective, and psychomotor content—that is, concepts, attitudes, and skills. Readers are welcome to complete their learning by participating in such a workshop offered by the Jubilee Popular Education Center in Raleigh, North Carolina. Jubilee is a small center where staff do research and training, teaching adult educators how to use popular education as we understand it.

Acknowledgments

This book is dedicated to Jubilee Fellows all over the world who have taken the Jubilee Introduction to Popular Education course. Their input and suggestions continually enhance Jubilee's work. I also want to celebrate the team at Jossey-Bass, especially Alan Knox and Gale Erlandson, who constantly manifest patience, courage, and wisdom in presenting accessible adult education research. Finally, I thank my colleague, sister, and good friend Joan Vella, who is the first among Jubilee Fellows and the best of first readers.

Raleigh, North Carolina   Jane Vella
                                                                August 1995

The Author

Jane Vella is president of Jubilee Popular Education Center in Raleigh, North Carolina, and adjunct professor at the School of Public Health, University of North Carolina, Chapel Hill. She received her B.A. degree (1955) from Rogers College in New York, her M.A. degree (1965) from Fordham University, and her Ed.D. degree (1978) from the University of Massachusetts, Amherst.

Vella has worked in community education in Africa, Asia, North and South America, and Europe since 1955. She has designed and led community education and staff development programs in more than forty countries around the world. During her tenure at Save the Children in the United States, she did the field research that resulted in the publication of her book *Learning to Teach* (1989). In 1994, Jossey-Bass published her first book on adult education, *Learning to Listen, Learning to Teach: The Power of Dialogue in Educating Adults*.

1

Teaching Adults

Insights from Popular Education

Conversion to the people requires a profound rebirth.
—Paulo Freire (1993, p. 43)

This chapter explores the assumptions and hypotheses of popular education, an approach to adult education that is based on a particular conception of what it means to be human, a sense of what the world is and can be, a view of the potential of community and society, and finally, a clear epistemology, that is, an understanding of how human beings learn. I will try to make explicit and clear these elements that underlie popular education by addressing four fundamental questions:

1. Who am I?
2. What is the world?
3. How can I live and work with others?
4. What is "to know"?

Who Am I?

The central question in western literature, from my point of view, was spoken by Shakespeare's King Lear: "Who is it will tell me who I am?" Any education theory assumes a satisfactory response to that fundamental question. Who are we? What does it mean to be human?

1

The concept of popular education was born in Latin America in the second half of the twentieth century. It is deeply related to other, older educational theories that hold a similar view of humankind as born to be free, to be subjects rather than objects, decision makers in their own lives, and makers of a world in which, as Paulo Freire put it, "it is easier to love" (1993, p. 22). One would, therefore, not expect this approach to learning to have been used in medieval Europe, where church leaders told men and women what their lives meant. One would not have dared to use popular education in apartheid South Africa of the 1970s, or in Hitler's Germany. Paulo Freire calls such societies "sectarian" and quotes the Brazilian journalist Marcio Moreiro Alves in describing them: "They suffer from an absence of doubt" (Freire, 1993, p. 21).

This assumption about the nature of human beings is operative throughout every moment of a popular education program. It is the reason, the rationale, for the simple techniques such as needs assessment, open questions, and small-group work that will be demonstrated in this book. At the beginning of the twentieth century Maria Montessori (1870–1952) worked from the same premise in honoring the development of infants. Her approach to preschool training sounds surprisingly like popular education for adults, because her assumptions about what people are and what they are for is so similar to the assumptions of popular education. Kurt Lewin, psychologist, proposed a system of motivation based on the assumption that men and women are indeed subjects of their own lives, making decisions that create their world (Lewin, 1951).

The assumption of human freedom and potential on which popular education is based is operative in and informs every element of the design of adult learning. When trainers' actions or the design of the training are incongruent with this assumption about humankind, it shows in the dis-ease of the learners, their reluctance to work, and their resistance to learning. Those who teach others how to use popular education are hoisted on their own petard, forced to be congruent with their own assumptions.

What Is the World?

In the popular education approach to adult education, the world in which we live, our particular society and its economical, political, social, ecological, and educational systems, is historically based. As Paulo Freire says, "[T]here is no historical reality which is not human. There is no history without humankind, and no history for human beings, there is only history of humankind, made by people and in turn, making them" (1993, p. 111). Our systems are open systems, susceptible to change. We human beings are made through our struggle to learn, through our efforts to re-create the complex world in which we live.

This process gives popular education its essential quality of openness, creativity, critical questioning, and dialogue. "To affirm that men and women are persons, and as persons should be free, and yet to do nothing tangible to make this affirmation a reality, is a farce" (Freire, 1993, p. 32). We accept the strenuous task of educating individuals to see the implications of their own perceptions, and we accomplish this by honoring those perceptions, listening to them, challenging them when necessary, and putting diverse perceptions into dialogue with one another. Donald Oliver (1989) reminds us that the observer is part of what he or she observes. As educators, we bring our own perception into any learning situation. While we owe ourselves the same respect we afford learners, we have to be conscious of the power of our unique and idiosyncratic perception when we are perceived as "the professor." This consciousness is at the base of our efforts, as educators of adults, to form relationships of trust and mutuality with adult learners. Freire (1993) assures us that adult learners will effect and celebrate this mutuality when they feel it is necessary.

Abraham Maslow's (1954) research posits a ladder of needs, showing physical and security needs that must be met before other "higher" needs can be addressed. These realities are all operative in the world, and educators must invite adults to examine them through problem-posing dialogue. Whether learning how to operate a television camera, or how to understand social systems in a sociology course, or to show respect to patients crowding into a rural clinic, one is also, on another level, learning a view of the world, and of humankind.

Popular education is based on this assumption that the world can be changed, that society, systems, and policies are open to alteration and renewal. This approach invites educators and adult learners alike to be scientists: to take a hypothesis and test it until the hypothesis and reality seem to agree. This approach to adult learning is not learning for its own sake. It is essentially inviting men and women to learn about the world as it is in order to make the world what it might be for them and their children. It invites people to learn as active subjects, as decision makers.

If this approach were being used in an adult education history course, for example, learners would be invited to question the facts presented, to re-present them from their own cultural perspective, to analyze the causes of conflicts and policies—essentially, to redesign the course with the teacher so that it reflects the learners' reality, which is in turn questioned and analyzed. If the popular education approach were used to teach a technical skill, learners would be invited to name other ways of doing a task, to investigate the ecological implications of the instruments they are learning to use, to imagine dangers and crises, and to think critically about the process and its results. Every learning event creates the world. By using popular education, the world created can reflect the themes and interests of the adult learners.

Freire's major work, *Pedagogy of the Oppressed* (1993), criticizes traditional education, which presents the world as a closed system belonging to a few who control the rest. He proposes an alternative approach—problem-posing education, or popular education—which invites adult learners to design a world that belongs to all human beings. A view of the world as an open system, amenable to change, is basic to the process of adult learning in this approach. The microworld created in a training workshop is shared, owned so to speak by all involved. The camaraderie and mutual respect created by the process is not peripheral to the process. It is based on the participants' shared assumption of what the world is, and what it might be in terms of who they are and who they are becoming.

An example of this "re-creation" can be seen in the final celebration of a group of twenty-four Chilean physicians, nurses, and social workers involved in a community health program near Santiago (see Chapter Three). They met for a first session of their new coalition on the last day of a train-the-trainer workshop, and each participant in the workshop invited one other professional who had not been in the workshop to share in the celebration. This was their Chilean interpretation of the principle of inclusion. It was designed to avoid any exclusivity right from the beginning of their health-workers coalition, among the men and women who had learned in the workshop how to do community education using the popular education approach. Their celebration reflected their desire to create a world without sectarianism.

Jung (1969) teaches that the purpose of human life is to become conscious. The popular education approach to adult learning invites optimal consciousness, to do what one is doing in the world as intentionally as possible. Imagine a world of mutual respect, with equitable distribution systems and adequate housing, where it is easier to love. It takes men and women who are subjects of their own lives to design and bring about such a world. We can begin that process in educational events and projects that manifest that kind of world. These two basic assumptions—about what human beings are and can become, and about the world as an open system—form the backbone of the hypothesis about adult learning that is popular education.

How Can I Live and Work with Others?

Assumptions about human beings and the world lead directly to assumptions about society. No one is truly alone in the world. In the popular education approach to adult learning, society is assumed to be the matrix for learning, the means for world building, an intentional gathering of subjects, free men and women who are decision makers in their own lives. In their effort to form a community, they individually make personal concessions to meet the needs of the community. The group itself becomes the subject, making decisions with the good of all in mind. These personal concessions are not easy. Often there are painful contradictions between the decisions of the individual and the needs of the group. As a microcosm, the adult learning situation mirrors this larger societal phenomenon: individuals making concessions for the learning of the group.

In the popular education approach, the teacher's role in the learning society is assumed to be that of servant, leader, sage, conductor, questioner, arbitrator, catalyst, and often decision maker. These roles are evident in every educational project that is based on the popular education, problem-posing approach. In this view, the teacher is closer to the shaman than to the professor, asking more often than telling, affirming more often than correcting, guiding and coaching more often than leading and training.

The congruence between the teacher's role in the wider society and in the microsetting of an educational event is a very important aspect of the total hypothesis of popular education. Freire (1993) showed that the teacher is also a student, and that the student is also a teacher. Dialogue, essential to popular education, invites all participants to both contribute and listen. When the teacher is not a listener but a teller, master, and critic, the learner can be reduced to dependency, and often anger. Freire calls this process oppression. If such oppression is not addressed in the educational event, how can it be met in the larger world? When education addresses oppression by using the popular education approach, it can become "the practice of freedom" (Freire, 1993). There is a notable new relationship between teacher and student when this approach is being used.

The structures of society are intentional, designed by subjects who are conscious of their own needs and aspirations. A broadly based misconception of popular education, in my perspective, is that it is an unstructured educational process—a broad invitation to the dance without any set music. On the contrary, form is not sacrificed when democracy emerges. In the microsetting of popular education for adults, a structure does exist. It is designed in dialogue, with respect for resources and needs. So, the perception of society as structured, diverse, open, and changing forms and informs the social aspects of popular education: honoring diversity; respecting each individual; using achievement-based objectives, small-group work, praxis (action with reflection), and action evaluation; being aware of the distinction between a consultative voice (suggestions) and a deliberative voice (decision making) in a group; and celebrating listening. Each person learns as an individual with and for others in a society. That is the assumption of popular education.

What Is "to Know"?

I sit here at my desk, working, alive, sensing the beautiful Carolina sunlight, because a laughing Italian youth "knew" a beautiful young Irish woman. That biblical knowing is passionate and creative. We also "know" facts, such as the date of Lincoln's birthday; skills, such as how to prepare a tasty dinner; and attitudes, such as how to listen to our teenage sons and daughters when they are confused. Such cognitive, psychomotor, and affective knowing can also be passionate and creative. Popular education, as understood in this book, assumes that passion and creativity are the stuff of human knowing, available to all men and women, available to any form of learning, in any situation.

Lincoln's date of birth, for example, is more than a fact. It is a time in history with vital surroundings: rough roads, a struggling democracy, a log cabin, flickering candlelight. His birth, and his life, full of creativity and passion, are not captured, however, by the simple concept of February 12, 1809. Concepts are never single or disassociated. Popular education honors concepts as integrated, historic, and always complex. They are then taught as such, with respect for their complexity.

The skills involved in the preparation of a tasty dinner, for example, are honored in a similar way. All of one's culture and history is at play when learning any skill, especially one as important as cooking. Fragrances, sounds, tastes, and the pain and joy of meals remembered are all involved. Popular education respects that historicity, and uses it in preparing to teach any complex skill. Attitudes are caught, not taught. Attitudes are often practiced as skills that have roots in the heart. A popular education approach honors the fact that new attitudes take time to become fully rooted, and long practice before they are fully integrated into a person's life.

Popular education respects the fact that skills, concepts, and attitudes are intertwined. People learn new actions, ideas, and feelings, and they also learn through ideas, actions, and feelings. Knowing is an active process, a political process in that it always involves power, and a dialogical process. A design for dialogue in popular education invites educators and learners to be constantly aware of the balance of power.

An epistemological framework—that is, as stated earlier, an understanding of how human beings learn—is always at work in the design and implementation of adult learning. The epistemology of popular education, as I see it, holds that knowing is a complex process involving the entire person. It is not only a cognitive task. Education is not merely sharing information. It needs to be physical, involving the muscles and skeletal system, and affective, involving the hormones and the heart. How can this be done when teaching parents of HIV-positive hemophiliacs how to care for their sick child, when teaching the basics of auto mechanics to an urban youth, when teaching ergonomics to truck drivers at a union meeting, when teaching basic anatomy to first year medical students? The need to answer these questions is why consideration of epistemology can be useful to adult educators.

The hypotheses examined in this chapter are clearly not unique to popular education. They are basic, commonsense assumptions about adult learning, derived from the sound research of the twentieth century: adult human beings are free subjects of their own lives; they can transform the world as they transform themselves; society can be structured for service and mutuality; and knowing is a complex process involving the whole self. If these are not unique to popular education, they *are*, however, explicit in the approach to adult learning known by that name. Insofar as they are found and practiced elsewhere in the world of educational theory and practice under other names, I rejoice. There is no proprietary issue here. The problem often faced in education comes from the obverse of these assumptions, which holds that individuals are neither free nor capable of being subjects; that they need direction; that the world is a given—nothing can be done about it; that society designs itself by virtue of an invisible hand; and that knowing is a matter of moving incontrovertible facts from the professor's page to the learner's. Under these assumptions, educators attempt to cover as much as they can in the given time, so they can transmit as much information as possible to learners. From the point of view of popular education, these assumptions are a dangerous basis for human learning.

I present therefore, in the chapters that follow, some ways of teaching adult educators and trainers to work from the hypotheses and assumptions of popular education described in this chapter. I begin in Chapter Two by examining a train-the-trainers program called Introduction to Popular Education that is based on these four assumptions.

2

Training Trainers in the Popular Education Approach

One Model

Education is constantly remade in the praxis.
—Paulo Freire (1993, p. 65)

This chapter presents one model for a week-long course in popular education. The seven steps of planning—who, why, when, where, what, what for, and how—that are taught in the course will be used here to show the design of the course. The model presented is generic. It is constantly being remade as it is used with different groups in different situations. It is my hope that readers will adapt this model to their own needs as they use it to design courses.

The Seven Steps of Planning

Seven questions need to be answered in the planning of this course.

1. *Who?* Asking this question invites a profile of the participants and the number expected. Participants could be individuals who do adult education and training and staff development in industry, in nonprofit groups, in community settings, in clinics, and in schools and colleges. The number of participants is a major factor. Working with eight to twelve participants has proved to be the most successful because, as you will see, the course involves practice design and microteaching. The time needed for such work precludes larger numbers of participants.

2.   *Why?* Answering this question reveals the situation that demands such training. The men and women who will be invited to participate are experienced trainers who recognize their need to enhance their skills, knowledge, and attitudes about adult learning. They are aware of the training needs in their own organizations or communities and of their need to design trainings to meet those needs, and they hope to be able to do so more successfully as a result of taking the course.

3.   *When?* Answering this question establishes the time frame. Experience has shown that thirty-five hours in five days is the most comfortable amount of time busy professionals can spend. There is also a need to make the week the first in a series of such events—for instance, Phase One of a four-phase curriculum of training.

4.   *Where?* Answering this question determines the site where the course will be given. The ideal setting would be a comfortable room with tables for small groups, a table for a small library setup, a flip chart and easel, and a VCR and monitor. Jubilee is fortunate to often hold the course at a quiet, rural retreat center that has a large comfortable room with a fireplace, tables for groups of four, and a circle of rocking chairs. The site is a dramatically important factor in the success of a training program.

5.   *What?* Answering this question determines the content of the course—the skills, knowledge, and attitudes (SKAs) to be taught. These may include the following:

Theory on how adults learn

Lewin's dozen principles for learning

The problem-posing approach: dialogue

The "banking" approach: monologue

Achievement-based objectives

Principles and practices of popular education

Cognitive, affective, and psychomotor aspects of learning

How to do a learning needs assessment

Generative themes of a community

Theory on how groups work

The seven steps of planning

How to design and use a warm-up

How to design problem-posing learning materials

How to ask open questions

Healthy attitudes for accountable learning

How to get and give feedback

How to evaluate the immediate and long-term indicators of
learning

The idea of the learner as subject and decision maker

Techniques for participative adult learning

6. *What for?* Answering this question identifies the achievement-based objectives. For example, by the end of the first five days all participants will have

Reviewed current *adult learning theory*

Distinguished between *monologue* (banking) and *dialogue*
(problem-posing) as approaches to learning

Practiced doing a *learning needs assessment*

Identified the *generative themes* of a group

Reviewed *how groups work* with optimal participation

Used and evaluated the principles and practices of popular
education

Practiced designing and using *open questions*

Practiced designing *learning sessions* in teams using the
principles and practices of popular education

Practiced designing *problem-posing learning materials* that
engage learners

Practiced teaching using their own design

Reviewed theory on *feedback,* and practiced giving and getting feedback on designs and teaching

Designed two *evaluation instruments:* one for immediate and one for long-term evaluation of their teaching

Read at least one book from the library of resources

Practiced consistent behavior expressing healthy attitudes, for example, critical thinking, collaboration, humor

Used a wide variety of *problem-posing teaching techniques*

These objectives are quantifiable and verifiable; we are therefore accountable to achieve them.

A fundamental concept throughout this course is *modeling*—we do what we are teaching. All of the achievement-based objectives are implemented through a design that models the problem-posing approach, that demonstrates the use of all the skills, knowledge, and attitudes being taught. The design itself is accountable for the effectiveness of the course. As you can see, the content and the objectives are closely linked. Achievement-based objectives are what the learners will *do* with the content in order to learn it. This correspondence is what makes the design *accountable,* and it is at the heart of the difference between popular education and traditional education, which speaks of "covering" content and uses such objectives as "to learn about . . . ," "to understand . . . ," and "to know. . . ." This model of popular education is very demanding in its specificity. Popular education as learner-centered adult education and training means that, by design, the learner is doing something with the content.

7.   *How?* Answering this question leads to the structure of the program, the learning tasks and materials to be used. The structure of the week-long program can be broken into five sections: preparation, introduction, theory, practice, and closure.

Preparation

The first preparation task of the course leader and designer is selection of participants. Guidelines for this task include determining potential participants' experience in the field of adult education, their transcultural experience, and whether they sense a strong need to enhance their theoretical base and practical skills.

As stated earlier, the designer of such a training course needs to control the number of participants to allow for adequate time for reflection, questions, design, and microteaching within the five-day framework. Designers may be tempted to decide on numbers based on economics. Be cautioned: more is not merrier in this case.

The next task is to survey the participants after they have reviewed the topics to be included (the *topical program*). They are asked to respond in writing to questions such as the following:

1. Why are you excited about taking this week-long course?
2. What have you read about adult learning that has helped you in your work?
3. What are your present teaching or work responsibilities, including current issues that you face?
4. What do you hope to have achieved and to have learned by the end of this training course?

This survey provides a profile of the twelve registered participants. It begins the dialogue. The choice of words is intentional. It assumes that they are reading. It assumes that they are pleased about the opportunity to participate in the course and that they have their own personal expectations which they will share. The information received from the survey does not form the course, but it significantly informs it. In each of the examples discussed in Chapters Three to Eight, the survey responses provided a great deal of information about the very diverse groups and enabled the planners to fit generic learning tasks to the group, where possible.

Such a learning needs assessment is also a resource assessment. You can imagine how important it is to discover that a prospective participant has studied with Alan Knox at Wisconsin, or done Peace Corps training for twenty years, or has recently read all the titles in the Jossey-Bass Higher Education series; or to discover that, as one person put it, "I leave the reading to others," or that a training director, a physician, at an international organization has never studied adult education. These are facts that simply must be known before the design is completed.

To design with the seven steps of planning is the next task in the preparation process, using the information about the "who" and their "why" and their expectations to adapt the generic design. Making materials, setting out the logistical framework—the site, the arrangement of the room, the charts and videos, the overhead projector, name cards, place cards, groupings—all of this takes time that is essential for accountable preparation of this popular education training course.

When considering the "who," it is important also to consider who will be the *trainers* or *instructors* for the workshop. I have discovered that I am much more accountable to the learners when I am in a teaching team of two. Lyra Srinivasan shares this insight: "The enabling function at a workshop is not an easy task. It is best entrusted to a team of two facilitators rather than one. Due to low budgets, project managers often try to get by with just one facilitator. I find this is a false economy. Unlike a lecture session where participants are largely passive, the high intensity and sensitivity of an interactive group process can be overwhelming for a lone trainer, even one highly experienced" (1992, p. 92). It is not merely a question of fatigue, although that is a serious consideration, but it is also a question of attention to the learners. As Mrs. Loman says in Arthur Miller's poignant *Death of a Salesman*, "Attention must be paid" (Miller, 1949, p. 56). Each adult learner, each adult trainee, is an individual, with specific, individual, personal needs. The number of trainees is controlled to give each person adequate airtime; the number of trainers must also be controlled to give learners adequate attention.

The last step in preparation is a quiet one: sitting still, keeping quiet, paying attention to the inevitable doubts and concerns that assail any trainer or educator before he or she steps out to meet the group. I personally always get "butterflies" before a course begins. It is nature's way, as I see it, to keep me aware of the responsibility I have to the learners, and to the program, and to myself. Without some quiet time before a program begins, this very natural nervousness can be visible to the group at the outset of the program.

Introduction

The course begins with a warm welcome by name to each of the adult learners. They are seated at tables of four, with a name card marking their place. Each participant is provided with a materials notebook containing all the learning tasks for the week, a set of cards with the fifty principles and practices of popular education, one on each card, and a set of cards containing the seven steps of planning. Charts of all the learning tasks for day one are stacked on an easel. Each learning task is an open question that will be put to the learners in small groups while providing them with the resources they need to respond. The learning tasks, as indicated in their notebooks, are tasks to be carried out by the participants, the learners, not by the instructor.

After a very brief introductory statement about the site and a statement that throughout the workshop the instructors will be *modeling* what they are teaching, Task 1, the warm-up, begins. This task is based on the need of a group of adults to focus and to clear their heads of the manifold concerns and interests that they bring to the course. The warm-up is a learning task; in this case, it demonstrates how important such a time of focusing is, and how useful it is to design a task that includes cognitive, psychomotor, and affective aspects. It teaches the group about the resources within the group, as individuals share symbols, using found objects, of their work in the world. This warm-up task happens to touch directly on the first two questions framing the assumptions of popular education: Who am I? and What is the world?

TASK 1: WARM-UP

Select a found object that symbolizes your work in the world. Put it on the table and share with your small group why you chose it, as you introduce yourself.

Notice that the dialogue has begun not between the instructor and the learners but among the learners. Rather than saying how things should be, the instructors can "make it so" by doing it. This is popular education: respecting the experience of the participants and their ability to respond at the symbolic level. There are an endless number of warm-ups to choose from (see Vella, 1989), and new forms can be constructed, but the one shown here is a favorite since it does invite a symbolic level of dialogue, and it clearly tests the assumption that the participants are willing to dialogue, to learn more about each other than facts and figures. I have not even once been in a group where individuals refused to do this task. Perhaps its charm is in its power to address the very first question in the assumptions: Who am I?

The next step in the introduction is a review of the stated objectives, the content, and the topical program. Copies of these are in the participants' notebooks, but charts of all three are also on the easel so they can be used by the instructors in their descriptions and to respond to requests for clarification. The learning tasks are set out in sharp, specific verbs—for example, read, identify, name, examine, and so forth.

TASK 2: PROGRAM REVIEW AND EXPECTATIONS

Read the objectives and the content and the topical program. What are your questions? At your table, describe your personal expectations of this week-long workshop. Write each expectation on a card, which will be posted here and shared with the whole group.

This task honors the learners' individuality and the idiosyncratic nature of learning. Each of the participants can read the same objectives, content, and program and see twelve different realities. When they name their personal expectations, their hopes and fears about the course, they are quietly celebrating themselves as subjects, or decision makers, in their own learning. The expectations are read aloud to the whole group after they are posted on a chart, and kept for review during the formative evaluation at the end of each day and in the final, summative evaluation at the end of the week. While these expectations, like the survey responses, do not form the program, they do *inform* the program. They are heard and heeded.

The introductory process will take a few hours. This initial dialogue must not be rushed, in keeping with the instructors' promise to model what they are teaching. It is vital for instructors to recognize that the introductory tasks are indeed learning tasks, that setting the environment for learning takes time, and that practicing dialogue among peers is a major part of the learning process in which each person is respected and heard.

Many adult learners find this dialogue approach somewhat strange and new. They need time to get comfortable with it and with the new role of the instructor: asking questions, not always answering them. Participants quickly relax and find their rhythm of working together on learning tasks. I have seen that energy rises as men and women work together, talking among themselves about their perceptions and their questions. In the same way, energy falls dramatically when a learning task is given to individuals to do alone. My reading of this phenomenon is that our first assumption, that men and women are born to be subjects of their own learning, can be expanded to say that we are intrinsically connected subjects. Joseph Campbell (Campbell and Moyers, 1988) reminds us that all around the world, people have the same bodies and therefore, the same myths. When that phenomenological connection is neglected, in a destructively competitive, solipsistic process focusing on individual activity and learning, adult learners lose their natural energy and begin to feel intimidated and alone. This is reason enough for me to demand small tables for group work, and to invite adult learners to work together on learning tasks, to use a popular education approach.

There is constant pressure in any adult learning situation to "cover" as much as possible in the allotted time. As said earlier, more is not merrier; on the contrary, less is more. Popular education is a serious process with a significant product. It is not a means of merely covering a curriculum. Accountability is the principle that assures the learners that both the instructors and the design will be accountable to them, and that the learners will be accountable to one another. (The quantity/quality issue will be addressed further in Chapter Eleven, on evaluation indicators.)

Theory

The next set of learning tasks invite participants to review basic theories of adult learning, beginning with Malcolm Knowles's (1980) research on how adults learn, as introduced in the following learning task:

TASK 3: HOW ADULTS LEARN

In pairs, describe the best learning experience in your life. Analyze it: What were the factors that made it so memorable and effective? Write each of the factors you name on these cards, one on a card, and post them on the chart entitled "Our Factors."

As we draw connections between the factors named by course participants in this inductive task, we create a web chart. Their factors are connected with lines and the final chart looks like a giant web. These web charts will be used throughout the training course as we do further brainstorming and share the results of small group dialogues. Web charts demonstrate how interconnected many factors are. After we review all the factors we compare them with those of Malcolm Knowles, who did research on adult learning. Knowles named four vital factors as prerequisites for effective adult learning: respect, immediacy, relevance, and the fact that adults retain

20 percent of what they hear, 40 percent of what they both hear and see, and 80 percent of what they do.

The dialogue around this task is often profound, as adult learners review their long experience of learning and select and analyze what Maslow (1954) calls a *peak experience*. Consider the fourth assumption: What does it mean to know something? The answer given by popular education is: to know is to do. This learning task invites doing, on an affective and cognitive level. The participants are teaching one another from their own esteemed life experience. The resources provided for learners to respond to this particular learning task are their own life experience and a summary of Knowles's research. In and through the ensuing dialogue, learners learn.

What is the role of the instructor at this moment? To sit still, to pay attention, to keep quiet. There is a great deal of existential tension here, since in fact the instructor at this moment has the role of a resource person to the learner. The learning task and the time frame have been set, the dialogue has begun. I have found that many teachers balk at the challenge of apparently doing nothing while learners learn. When they complain, I invite two reflections: First, imagine what would happen if you hovered over every group and guided their dialogue toward what you know to be the right answer to the question, How do adults learn? Second, think of a coach or mentor who lays out the task for the dancer or singer or baseball player and gets them started. Think also of a laboratory situation in which students are engaged in structured experiments under the attentive gaze of a teacher. I also share the following axiom with uneasy instructors who are feeling a loss of control in the face of the challenge of learners' autonomy: men and women will only learn how to be autonomous by using their autonomy.

The popular education process involves a new relationship between the teacher and the adult learner. It is not an easy relationship, since it assumes that adult learners are subjects or decision makers in their own learning. The design for dialogue corroborates that assumption and enables the new relationship. It clearly indicates what the learners are to do together in order to learn.

The next learning theory to be reviewed is what is called *Lewin's dozen*.

TASK 4: LEWIN'S DOZEN

Listen to this lecture describing the work of Kurt Lewin at Cornell University. Select for study two of Lewin's dozen theories, or principles, of adult learning. Each principle is followed by a short explanation and by some application tasks. At your table, teach the others the two principles you selected. Ask any questions necessary for clarification.

Group members are provided with the following materials with which to work: a summary of Lewin's work set out as principles (in italics), with a short explanation following each principle and examples of situations that test the principle. This summary of Lewin's principles is the work of Johnson and Johnson, in *Joining Together* (1991).

THE PRINCIPLES OF KURT LEWIN

PRINCIPLE 1

Effective learning will affect the learner's cognitive structures, attitudes, values, perceptions, and behavioral patterns. That is, it always involves cognitive, affective, and psychomotor factors.

To learn to be a more effective chef, for example, the learner must develop a *concept* of what cooking is, positive *attitudes* toward all the procedures involved in cooking, *perceptions* that new actions involved in good cooking are appropriate to the context, and the belief that one is capable of performing the *skills* needed.

Consider this first principle applied to:

- Buying, cooking, and eating for better nutrition
- Playing the piano
- Planting a vegetable garden

PRINCIPLE 2

People will believe more in knowledge they have discovered themselves than in knowledge presented by others.

Lewin was a great believer in experimental procedures whereby a person behaviorally validates or disproves a theory. He believed that such procedures need to be introduced into the educational process so that students can test alternative behavioral patterns within controlled conditions. An approach to learning based on inquiry and discovery has been found to increase students' motivation to learn and their commitment to implement their conclusions in the future.

How can we invite critical consideration of such topics as:

- The usefulness of affirmation in training literacy volunteers
- The value of cross-cultural education in volunteer training
- The type ideas of the Myers-Briggs Type Indicator
- The importance of specific indicators for valid evaluation

PRINCIPLE 3

Learning is more effective when it is an active rather than a passive process.

When a learner can take a theory, concept, or practice and "try it on for size," he or she will understand it more completely, integrate it more effectively with past learning, and retain it longer. Most concepts are never really learned until one uses them.

What can a learner "do" with the following skill, knowledge, and attitude in order to learn them?

- Reading a new language
- History of the Vietnam war
- Uses of respect in adult education

PRINCIPLE 4

Acceptance of new ideas, attitudes, and behavioral patterns cannot be brought about by a piecemeal approach. One's whole cognitive/affective/behavioral system has to change.

The three elements are interconnected, and they change as a whole rather than as separate parts. Like any system, a cognitive/affective/behavioral system demands coherence, consistency, orderliness, and simplicity. Trying to change part of the system will not be effective. The need for consistency creates resistance to the item-by-item approach to learning. Only when the whole system changes will the learning be fully accepted and integrated.

How would this principle affect:

- A stress reduction program
- Teaching office staff to recycle paper products

PRINCIPLE 5

It takes more than information to change ideas, attitudes and behavioral patterns.

Telling people about the desirability of change does not mean that they will change. Providing a rationale for change is not sufficient to motivate people to change. Reading a book or listening to a lecture does not necessarily result in mastery or retention of the material, does not necessarily promote attitude change, and does not necessarily increase social skills.

Information often does generate interest in learning more about the desired change.

What alternatives do we have to *telling?*

What does this principle tell me about my own history of education?

When do people really *know they know?*

PRINCIPLE 6

It takes more than firsthand experience to generate valid knowledge.

Lewin stated that thousands of years of human experience with falling bodies did not bring humans to a correct theory of gravity. Besides experience, there needs to be a theoretical system that the experience tests out, and reflection on the meaning of that experience.

"Nothing is so practical as a good theory!" What does that mean to you in terms of this principle?

PRINCIPLE 7

Behavior changes will be temporary unless the ideas and attitudes underlying them are changed.

New behavioral skills may be practiced and mastered, but without changes in the person's ideas and attitudes, the new behavior patterns will fade away.

Give one example of that phenomenon in your own learning history. How does this principle apply to learning:

- Different nutritional practices
- Cross-cultural differences related to health practices
- Team-building skills
- Levels of playing a musical instrument

PRINCIPLE 8

*Changes in perception of oneself and one's social
environment are necessary before changes in ideas,
attitudes, and behavior will take place.*

Learners must perceive themselves as capable of doing the
needed behaviors and must see the behaviors as being appropriate to the situation before they will engage in them. Lewin
recognized that behavior, ideas, and attitudes are all steered by
perception. Your perceptions of yourself and your immediate
situation affect how you behave, what you believe, and how
you feel.

What does this principle say to you about any skill building you have done?

How can we as teachers develop healthy, appropriate self-
perception in learners of all ages?

How do you control your own self-perception in times of
crisis or depression or fear?

PRINCIPLE 9

*The more supportive, accepting and caring the social
environment, the freer a person is to experiment with new
behaviors, attitudes, and ideas.*

As the need to justify oneself and protect oneself against
rejection decreases, it becomes easier to experiment with new
ways of behaving, thinking, and valuing.

What does this mean to our first responsibility as teachers,
to respect the learner?

When did you ever feel free enough to experiment?

What kinds of systems do we need within our organizations to maintain this principle?

PRINCIPLE 10

For changes in behavior patterns, attitudes, and ideas to be permanent, both the person and the social environment have to change.

The person's role definitions, the expectations held by colleagues and friends, and the general values of career and social setting must all change if the person is to maintain changed behaviors, attitudes, and ideas. One of the reasons team training is often more effective than individual training is because it changes individuals and their social environment at the same time.

Using this principle, share ways you would deal with the following case study: There has been substantial turnover among the trainers of lay volunteers in your nonprofit organization. You are located in an area with many nonprofit organizations that train volunteers and cannot compete in terms of salary and benefits. The remaining staff are very stressed and pessimistic. Two new trainers have been hired and the administrative staff are anxious to get them out "into the field" as soon as possible. You are in charge of their orientation.

PRINCIPLE 11

It is easier to change a person's ideas, attitudes, and behavioral patterns when he or she accepts membership in a new group. The discussion and agreement that take place within a group provide a personal commitment and encouragement for change that is not present when only one person is being changed.

What group have you belonged to that shows you the validity of this principle? Describe your experience of learning within that group. What difference do you think it would have made in your learning if you had not been a member of that group?

PRINCIPLE 12

A person accepts a new system of ideas, attitudes, and behavioral patterns when he or she accepts membership in a new group. New groups with new role definitions and expectations for appropriate behavior are helpful in educational efforts. A person becomes socialized by internalizing the normative culture of the groups to which he or she belongs. As the person gains membership in a new group, a new normative culture is accepted and internalized.

How could your "membership" in this workshop affect your behavior as an educator?

What do your understand by "normative culture"?

As individual learners work with two of these twelve principles, and share theirs with the colleagues at their table, they begin to recognize how what is happening in the course rings true to what Lewin discovered in his research. They also find their energy rising as through the learning tasks they honor their own capability to interpret and apply Lewin's philosophy.

Again, the instructor's role is unique here. He or she is a resource person, setting the stage by a lecture describing Lewin's work, setting the task and the time frame, and responding to questions that arise from each table. The learners do the work, actively engaged and autonomously learning.

The design for dialogue is this education model's alternative to "telling." One of the axioms of popular education is, *Remember, most adult learners can read.* This learning task assumes that the men and women who are participating in the course can read, and invites them to learn by doing just that. The experience of learning Lewin's dozen is often the high point of the course. Individuals resonate with these twelve principles, and as they do the application tasks, they recognize anew how useful the principles are.

This activity is an example of how to teach a mass of cognitive material using the principles and practices of popular education.

Table groups are teaching one another a significant sample of the twelve principles; each person is the subject of his or her own learning as he or she interprets and applies Lewin's principles and then shares his or her learning with colleagues; all participants are highly engaged. All twelve of Lewin's principles are reviewed in a synthesis activity at the end of the task, going one by one through the twelve and inviting each person's interpretative response.

By studying both Lewin and Knowles, and in the review of their own best learning experiences, the participants have thoroughly reviewed current adult learning theory. The next task invites them to review the four assumptions and the short summary statement of popular education.

TASK 5: POPULAR EDUCATION

Read the following summary of some of the basic elements of popular education. What are your questions? What would you add? What would you change?

BASIC ELEMENTS OF POPULAR EDUCATION

What is popular education? In Latin America, following the seminal work of Brazilian educator Paulo Freire, churches and health groups began to design their educational work with communities as a *dialogue*. They called this *educación popular* to distinguish it from traditional schoolroom education and traditional adult education. In other parts of the world, this approach is often called nonformal education. In any case, it is characterized by certain transcultural traditions:

Participation of the learners in determining what is to be learned

Dialogue between learner and teacher and among learners

Small-group work to engage learners and to make explicit their context and their understanding of the causes of the problems they face

Visual support and psychomotor involvement

Accountability: "How do they know they know?"

Participative evaluation of results of programs

Respect for learners and teachers

A listening attitude on the part of teachers and resource people

Learners *doing* what they are learning

The following learning tasks teach practices of popular education: assessing learning needs, identifying generative themes, using ideas, actions, and feelings in all designs, distinguishing monologue and dialogue, maintaining and nourishing the small learning groups.

TASK 6: LEARNING NEEDS ASSESSMENT

1. In your table groups, examine the triangle model for assessment of learning needs and resources (Figure 2.1).
2. Consider how the learning needs and resources assessment was done for this workshop: telephone calls, written survey, gathering of participants' expectations in Task 2. What would you have added to make the learning needs assessment more complete?
3. What would you add to or change in the model?

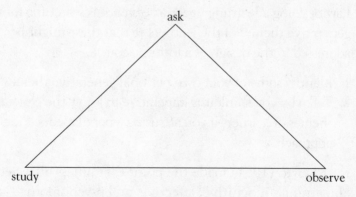

FIGURE 2.1. Learning Needs Assessment Model.

Again, the participants learn the model by using it. They review what the course planners did with them as an application of the model, and on the basis of their own perspectives, add to the learning needs assessments tasks. When learners are editing any model or a set of data, they are learning it.

Using the learning needs assessment model will afford you access to the themes of the people you will be teaching. Paulo Freire uses the term "generative themes" (1993) to show that these themes generate energy. He says "I must re-emphasize that the generative theme cannot be found in people divorced from reality, nor in reality, divorced from people; much less in 'no man's land'. It can only be apprehended in the human-world relationship. To investigate the generative theme is to investigate people's thinking about reality and people's action upon reality which is their praxis" (1993, p. 87).

TASK 7: IDENTIFYING GENERATIVE THEMES

Read the following short description, marking it with your questions and comments:

What are *generative themes?* Generative themes are ideas, problems, joys, and issues that generate energy within the individual. They "exist in people in their relations with the world, with reference to concrete facts" (Freire, 1993, p. 87). Part of doing a learning needs assessment is searching for the generative themes of the learners so that these might be addressed in the design of a training course.

1. Identify some of your own personal generative themes.
2. Tell why you think it is imperative to know the generative themes of learners if you are using a popular education approach.

Kurt Lewin (1951) made the point that unless all aspects of learning—cognitive, affective, and psychomotor—are considered, the result is less than it might be. In this next learning task, these three aspects are considered and applied to a critical incident, a case study that poses a clear problem.

TASK 8: COGNITIVE/AFFECTIVE/PSYCHOMOTOR ASPECTS OF LEARNING

Examine the Three Aspects of Learning symbol (Figure 2.2).

1. All learning can use all three aspects of learning: ideas (cognitive), feelings (affective), and actions (psychomotor). How have you seen us try to use all three in this course so far?
2. Read the following critical incident. Decide at your table how Kate Farrell could use the three factors to enhance her teaching. What else could she use from this popular education approach?

KATE FARRELL'S DILEMMA

Kate Farrell is a nurse in the Appalachian area of Kentucky. She has been teaching a group of mothers about infant nutrition and the use of their babies' growth charts to monitor health and development.

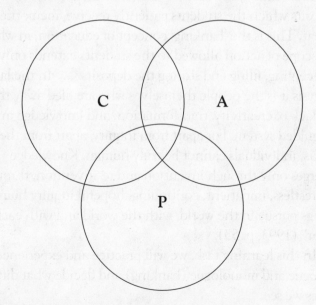

FIGURE 2.2. Three Aspects of Learning.

The fifteen women she is working with do not read or write. They have never been to school. Kate Farrell is telling them all that she learned about nutrition and using growth charts in her nursing school classes, but they do not seem to get it!

Kate thinks the mothers are all pretty stupid. Why can't they understand and demonstrate to her how they can feed their babies from all the food groups, and how they can tell from the growth charts whether their child is doing well or not? Instead, they sit there like lumps, nodding respectfully, nursing their babies, not learning a thing!

TASK 9: MONOLOGUE/DIALOGUE: TWO APPROACHES TO ADULT LEARNING

In *Pedagogy of the Oppressed,* Paulo Freire presents two contradictory stances: one he calls "banking" education, the other he calls problem-posing education, or dialogue. He says: "Education is suffering from narration sickness. . . . Education thus becomes an act of depositing, in which the students are the depositories and the teacher is the depositor. Instead of communicating, the teacher offers communiqués, and makes deposits which the students patiently receive, memorize and repeat. This is the 'banking' concept of education, in which the scope of action allowed to the students extends only as far as receiving, filing and storing the deposits. . . . In the last analysis it is the people themselves who are filed away through the lack of creativity, transformation, and knowledge in this misguided system. For apart from inquiry, apart from the praxis, individuals cannot be truly human. Knowledge emerges only through invention and re-invention, through the restless, impatient, continuing, hopeful inquiry human beings pursue in the world, with the world and with each other" (1993, p. 53).

In this learning task, we will practice and experience both dialogue and monologue (banking) and decide what differences we see.

1. *Dialogue*. Put the seven cards that contain the seven steps of planning into the order you as a group agree is most useful when planning an educational event. When you have completed this step, go around and look at what other table groups have agreed upon.

Groups have a great time with this task, arguing back and forth about the appropriate order, giving all sorts of reasons and rationales for their choice. Finally, they make a decision, but all participants come to see how context determines even the choice of the sequence of the planning questions. In one training session, at one point a group was ready to explore what other tables had done and one man surreptitiously moved the series of cards into the sequence he had been advocating. He had the good grace to chuckle at his own possessiveness. His group did not laugh.

Any number of questions arise in this dialogue; for example: What are SKAs? What is meant by "the situation"? What are achievement-based objectives? How do the "what" and the "what for" differ? To answer the last question I can usually send participants back to the planning steps for the course they are attending and show how the content (the "what") is usually a set of nouns while the achievement-based objectives (the "what for") are a set of verbs that tell what participants will do with that content. Remember, the purpose in this learning task is not to teach the seven steps of planning, but to teach the difference between monologue and dialogue. The seven steps are the means to that end.

2. *Monologue*. Listen to the presentation of the seven steps of planning. Write down your questions or comments.

At this point, I use a flip chart and put up the cards containing the seven steps of planning in the order I want participants to learn:

Who: number of participants

Why: the situation that calls for this training. (They need....)

When: the time frame

Where: the site

What: the SKAs

What for: the achievement-based objectives

How: the program tasks and materials

I give examples from my own teaching experience, but do not field any questions or comments. The group always goes slack during this monologue, becoming passive listeners, often taking notes. Those who had arranged the seven cards in the way I have indicated smile slyly, knowing they were "right." Others glower with indignation at the sudden change in the pace and mode of the course. I try not to overdo the "role play" of the "banking" teacher offering a monologue. However, the participants feel a marked difference from their previous experience of dialogue.

3. *Differences between dialogue and monologue.* At your table, identify the differences you felt in that experience between dialogue and monologue.

A rich dialogue usually ensues, as advantages and disadvantages appear for both approaches. The instructors emphasize that monologue works—people do learn via monologue. What and how they learn is vitally different, however, from the experience of dialogue. The political issues arise here with great clarity. After completing this task, participants can attest to the difference between the two approaches. This task is a wonderful example of inductive learning, that is, moving from an experience to the theory behind it.

The learners in this course have been working in small groups all day. The next learning task invites them to consider how they can keep their small group healthy. It invites them to reflect on how they have been taking diverse roles all day, and on how those roles interact.

TASK 10: HOW GROUPS WORK

Examine this model (Figure 2.3) of how groups work. The bicycle indicates that any group works on two wheels: task maintenance and group maintenance.

Now look at the various roles for each "wheel." Consider who in your small group you saw take these various roles today.

What other roles would you add to this short list?

Why is it vital for any group to have both "wheels" in motion?

As table groups examine their own work together, they not only learn the model, they also use it, and by using it, they truly learn it, thus using the process of praxis. By examining their own behavior on this first day in terms of the model, they see how they can

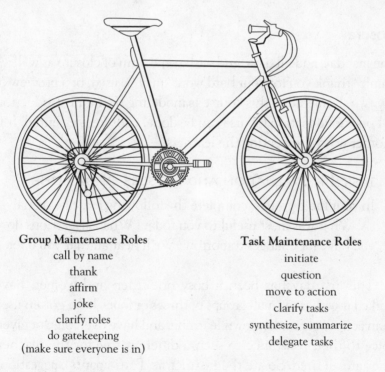

Group Maintenance Roles
call by name
thank
affirm
joke
clarify roles
do gatekeeping
(make sure everyone is in)

Task Maintenance Roles
initiate
question
move to action
clarify tasks
synthesize, summarize
delegate tasks

FIGURE 2.3. How Groups Work.

enhance their group work on day two by using the model to change some of their behavior in the group, for instance, by calling people by name, by gatekeeping, by summarizing, and by clarifying tasks.

Each day of the course ends in formative evaluation, that is, a process that invites the participants' response to the day via a force-field analysis tool. This asks them to identify the positive forces, and the negative ones.

+	−
What was most useful to you today?	What would you suggest we change?

This is called formative evaluation because the results can form, and reform, the course on day two.

Closure

The first day, and all days, end with some form of closure as well. A simple "thank you for your hard work" may be used, or a preview of day two. Remember, this course is modeling how an Introduction to Popular Education Course can be done. Closure is essential. It is another way of respecting the learners.

TASK 11: EVALUATION AND CLOSURE OF DAY ONE

In your table groups, complete the following force field analysis: What was most useful to you today? What suggestions do you have for changes tomorrow? We'll hear all that you offer.

The first day has been a busy one. Men and women have worked together in small groups of threes or fours, have gotten used to an active role in their own learning, and have overcome or given voice to their resistance to such a different role for the teacher. They are all tired. So are the instructors. Participants' suggestions in the formative evaluation of the first day will be honored and implemented as far as possible on the second day, to confirm their faith in the process. The distinction between the consultative (suggestion) voice and the deliberative (decision making) voice always holds, however. While it is the teacher's job to listen to participants' suggestions in the evaluation of day one and to use these suggestions where possible to inform the rest of the week's program, it is also clearly the teacher's job to decide what is to be taught and learned.

Participative processes in education do not mean that everyone decides what will be learned and how it will be learned. While the teacher/student dilemma is addressed in popular education, the roles are *not* interchanged. The teacher learns, as teacher; the student teaches, as student. I find the concept of participation clarified and enhanced by this distinction between the consultative and deliberative voices.

Day Two

The second day of the workshop begins with the following task:

TASK 12: WELCOME AND WARM-UP

Put it to music! Using as many of the principles and practices of popular education cards as you can, design and perform a song stating what you see as the basic premise of popular education.

This is a rousing warm-up. When I facilitate this, I perform an example, with piano accompaniment if possible, to give the groups courage. My performance is usually so outrageous in its use of rhyme and melody that the participants' laughter awakens their own sleeping muses. I have heard rap songs, lyrics sung to the melodies of folk music and patriotic tunes, and bad verse and dreadful rhythms, all accompanied by laughter and cheers at their own creativity. This activity is fun, it is practice in small group work, and it is creative and spontaneous learning. One axiom I teach is, if there is no laughter, there is little learning. This first task of the second day assures us that there is some real learning going on.

This is also the context in which to examine the issue of trivializing. This first task of day two does not trivialize what participants have been learning; on the contrary, the task honors their learning. Any trivialization—that is, mocking the content or the process—destroys the learning potential of adults. Mockery is not joy; it is not followed by healthy laughter. I must confess to a fury that erupts whenever I hear what I consider a trivializing remark or a trivializing task. As Mr. Keating in the film *Dead Poets Society* says to a student he is moving to new heights of feeling, "We are not laughing at you, son, we are laughing near you." What is trivializing fails to respect.

The next task, dealing with open questions, is perhaps the most important skill learned in this course. I always preface this task by stating that on my deathbed, when asked to give my message to the world, I shall whisper, "Ask open questions." Open questions are the heart of the magic of participative, problem-posing, accountable adult education.

TASK 13: OPEN QUESTIONS INVITE DIALOGUE

1. Read the following questions. Tell the others at your table what you see as the difference between open questions and closed questions.

Do you like this workshop?

How can I help you?

What have you found is the best way to give this injection?

What is your middle name?

What was the best session in this workshop for you?

How will you use this new way of teaching?

2. The following are closed questions. At your table, tell how you would make each of them an open question.

Do you like this workshop?

Is this a good setting for the workshop?

Would you prefer coffee or tea?

Are you well?

Are there any questions?

3. Design one open question you might use to invite dialogue. Share it at your table and with the large group.
4. Examine the following four open questions, which move the discussion through (a) description, (b) analysis, (c) application, and finally, (d) implementation of change. Do you see that this is praxis? Go back to Kate Farrell's dilemma in Task 7. Use these questions to work again with that critical incident. What use do you perceive the open questions are to your learning?

What do you see happening here? (description)

Why do you think it happens? (analysis)

When it happens in your situation, what problems will it cause? (application)

What can be done to improve such a situation? (implementation of change)

In the next task, participants are invited to examine a sample design that synthesizes all the SKAs they have been learning about learning.

TASK 14: A SAMPLE DESIGN

1. Read the following sample design, marking it as you read. Record your questions.
2. Note the use of the seven steps of planning. What are your questions about the order and meaning of each step?

3. Name one task you would do differently if you were teaching this event. Tell why. We'll respond to all questions from all tables, and we'll hear all changes.

A SAMPLE POPULAR EDUCATION DESIGN

This is a sample of a one-hour workshop using the seven steps of planning and all the principles and practices we have been reviewing.

1. *Who?* All of the thirty participants, volunteers in a literacy organization, are always at meetings; they have indicated a need for this training.
2. *Why?* These participants need to analyze the problems they have at meetings and to make the meetings more effective.
3. *When?* For sixty minutes during a four-day-long annual conference.
4. *Where?* In a hotel conference room with tables of four.
5. *What?* All the substantive items in the checklist on how to have an effective meeting agenda; inclusion; deliberative/consultative votes; environment.
6. *What for?* By the end of the sixty minutes, participants will have identified problems they face in meetings, analyzed a case study presenting many of those problems, and examined a checklist for having a good meeting, adding to the list and identifying which are most useful to their own situation.
7. *How?* Learning tasks, as in the following program materials: a case study of a critical meeting; a checklist.

THE PROGRAM

Task i: Needs Assessment. Name at least three problems you have in meetings. Share them at your table and then write all that you have mentioned on cards and put them on the chart entitled "Common Problems We Have at Meetings."

Task ii: A Critical Meeting. Read the following story about a troubled meeting in Chicago. Use these four open questions. We'll hear your response to the first three questions.

What do you see happening here? (description)

Why do you think it happens? (analysis)

When it happens in your situation, what problems will it cause? (application)

What can be done to improve such a situation? (implementation of change)

WE'VE GOT TO STOP MEETING LIKE THIS! Here is a typical situation in a busy not-for-profit agency in a large midwestern city. A critical meeting has been called for 4:00 P.M. by the director. He announced the meeting at the 11:00 coffee break that morning. It is Friday, December 19.

The director has prepared an agenda. It has twelve items on it! When people arrive at 4:00, somewhat reluctantly, they discover that the director is not present. He was called to a critical meeting by the chair of the board.

The meeting finally begins at 4:20 when the director arrives, a bit breathless from running. He does not have the materials he needs to distribute to staff for item 1 on his agenda.

A resource person has been invited to discuss budget problems with the staff. This budget specialist has not been briefed adequately. She does not understand that decisions on budget are made not by the staff but by the director and the board.

The writing on the blackboard is hardly legible because the room is dark on this wintry Friday late afternoon. No one has been designated recorder of the meeting, so when the blackboard is erased, the many points recorded there are lost.

The meeting ends abruptly when the director is called out for an important phone call from the Hewlett Foundation

about a proposal due to them on Monday. There is no indication when the group will meet again.

People go home quite frustrated.

Task iii: A Checklist. Read over this checklist for the preparation, facilitation, and recording of a meeting. Circle those
numbered items that would have helped the participants
make the meeting just described more effective. We'll share a
sample of your responses.

Preparation

1. Does everyone who should be at the meeting know about it
   well in advance?
2. Has an agenda been shared beforehand with all who are to
   be involved in the meeting? How long beforehand?
3. Is the meeting really necessary, or could the information be
   shared in another, less-expensive way?
4. Have the resource people been fully informed as to the
   participants, the purpose of the meeting, the time allotted,
   and their expected purpose in the meeting?
5. Does everyone have minutes of the last meeting, so there is
   continuity?
6. Have all the materials for the meeting been gathered, that
   is, documents, audiovisual support, and so forth?
7. Is the time set for the meeting appropriate, that is, the hour
   of the day, the day of the week, and so forth?
8. Is the time available for the meeting long enough for the
   issues that are to be raised?

Facilitation

9. Is it clear who the chairperson or facilitator of the meeting is?
10. Is the agenda available to all present?
11. Does everyone present have all the necessary materials for
    the meeting?

12. Are people clear about the difference between a consultative voice (a suggestion) and a deliberative voice (a decision)?

13. Has a recorder or secretary been appointed to keep a record of the meeting?

14. Is the meeting room adequate, that is, is the light good? Is there enough space? Enough table room? A blackboard, easel, and flip chart? Audiovisual apparatus?

15. How does the facilitator or chairperson assure brisk movement from agenda item to agenda item?

16. How does the group deal with an obtrusive member? A pair of obtrusive members? (Obtrusive means interfering, someone who is not cooperating with the process of the meeting.)

17. Are all of the participants feeling good about their opportunity to speak during the meeting? That is, is the meeting fully open?

18. How are questions for clarification asked? How about substantive questions on the issue? Do people see the difference?

19. Is the chairperson clear about which issues will be discussed for clarification only (informative)? For all to decide (deliberative)? For suggestions (consultative)?

20. Is the time sufficient for all of the tasks on the agenda?

21. How is the synthesis or summary to be done? Who will do it?

22. How is closure to be achieved?

Documentation

23. How soon is the recorder's report of the meeting given to the chair?

24. Are action decisions clearly taken and time lines set for completing actions?

25. How is the meeting linked with the next one?

26. What system exists to get the record of the meeting to all participants and to those who could not be present?

27. How is the evaluation of the meeting conducted?

Task iv: Application to Participants' Meetings. At your table, tell the others which item on this list is most important for your meetings. What would you add to the list? We will share all that you offer.

Task v: Synthesis and Evaluation: How Do You Know You Know?
1. Examine the objectives for this sixty-minute program and the content. What strikes you?
2. Take the snow cards off the board if you feel the problems you raised were addressed by what you learned.
3. What will you do differently as you design your next meeting? We'll share a sample of responses.

Dialogue around this sample design serves to make the seven steps of planning a more accessible tool for participants. Their knowledge of it, however, is still cognitive. Time after time, I have seen that this and other tools, practices, and principles do not become clear until the participants actually use them in their own design and microteaching.

So much that is fruitful and clarifying occurs during team design and teaching that a constant dilemma for me is, How soon can we start such microteaching? Lyra Srinivasan, in her classic designs for training trainers in Africa and Asia (1992), makes the entire program a design task for small teams, incorporating the theory in the interstices, so to speak. I would be grateful to hear from readers who have tried a different approach or have different views on this dilemma. My own predilection, reflected in the design presented in this book, is to consider safety a primary principle and to guide the participants slowly toward the design stage and toward their teaching. I would love to be proven wrong in this and learn how to do the design task earlier in the course.

Over the years I have gathered some axioms about adult learning and popular education. Examining this list of axioms and adding to it is a delightful means of summarizing all that the participants in this training course have learned so far.

TASK 15: AXIOMS OF POPULAR EDUCATION

1. Read the following set of axioms of popular education. "Axiom" is defined by *Merriam Webster's New Collegiate Dictionary*, Tenth Edition (1994), as "an established rule or principle or a self-evident truth." At your table, explain which one speaks most clearly to you and why. We'll share all.
2. What other axioms would you add to this set?

AXIOMS OF POPULAR EDUCATION

1. Don't tell what you can ask; don't ask if you know the answer—tell, in dialogue!
2. A warm-up is a learning task related to the topic.
3. You can't teach too little; you can't go too slowly.
4. A learning task is an open question put to a small group along with the resources they need to respond to it.
5. Don't write on a chart anything you won't use again.
6. A critical incident (a case study posing a problem) needs to be far enough away to be safe, close enough to be immediate.
7. The learning task is a task for the learner.
8. Pray for doubt!
9. If you don't dispute it, you don't learn it.
10. The more teaching, the less learning.

These axioms are a stimulating means of starting a dialogue on the theory and practice of popular education. One elderly professor at a recent seminar suggested he would use one axiom—If you don't dispute it, you won't learn it—to dispute all of them. This led to an enlightening sharing of perspectives.

Practice

TASK 16: DESIGN IN PAIRS

1. Select a partner with whom you wish to work.
2. Decide on a topic one of you wants to teach the group. The other person in the pair will have a chance to name his or her issue in the second microteaching.

3. Design together a learning needs and resources assessment instrument to discover what the learners already know and need or want to know about what you will teach.

4. Using the seven steps of planning and all the principles and practices, design together a forty-minute lesson. Design all the learning materials you need. The lesson will begin with a warm-up task and end with a closure task.

This is the heart of this course. It is a task that serves not only as a synthesis activity of all the cognitive learning that has taken place, but also as an opportunity to practice new skills and attitudes. It is very important that the participants do this task in pairs. They have worked in learning teams throughout the course. Now they must supply their own task and group maintenance resources to nourish their design teams.

The time factor is very important here. The usual ratio of preparation time to teaching time for a popular education design is three to one. Teams are invited to complete their design, including their learning needs assessment, in three hours, since they will be teaching for about one hour.

The learners in this microteaching session are the other ten participants in the training course. They are themselves, and are not asked to play a role for the sake of the microteaching. My experience proves that teaching one's peers as themselves is a true situation, a real challenge. If they were asked to role play as another group of people, the "learners'" ability to act would be a new factor in an already complex situation.

Before beginning this task, instructors should have participants brainstorm topics for teaching, asking individuals to write on cards what they would like to teach the group and put these on a board so all participants can respond to them. If a nurse wants to teach the group about universal precautions against AIDS, or an insurance salesman wants to explain reverse mortgages, or a TV specialist wants to teach the group how to use a video camera effectively, participants can indicate their level of interest by checking for or against that topic. This is a simple way of priming the pump so that teams do not spend an inordinate amount of time deciding what to teach.

I urge teams to use the sample design they reviewed in Task 14 as a guide, to consider how their materials are problem posing, to write learning tasks for the learners. I ask them to promise that they will *not stay stuck*. That is, they are invited to call the instructors in at any time in the process for a "consultation."

This is an intimidating learning task, and it is a difficult time for all participants. There is a strong sense of healthy competition, with everyone wanting to do it well the first time. There is always a sense of being overwhelmed by the complexity of the process and the multiplicity of factors to consider. It does not help for the instructor to say, "This is only a practice session." I have learned that there is no way to help people over the hump of fear and inadequacy except by being there as a resource.

Structuring in two design and microteaching sessions in a training course instead of only one has revealed the power of this experiential learning. The quality of both the second design time and of the second microteaching is immensely superior to the quality of the first ones. Experience and reflection are good teachers.

What is the task of the instructor in all this? As named earlier, it is to sit still, to pay attention, and to keep quiet. The participants' working through the task independently is their way to learning, and any uninvited "help" from the instructor can stop that difficult and efficacious process. Long ago I realized that all learning is idiosyncratic and immensely personal. I cannot learn for another human being, and I can interfere with the process of his or her idiosyncratic learning by trying to help. I insist that all consultations be specific, that is, that the team name their immediate problem, and I respond specifically to it. For example, a team may say: "Help us. We feel this is too much to try to teach in forty minutes. What do you think?" I review their objectives and content, give my opinion and some specific suggestions, and then leave. The leaving is indubitably my best gift to the design team.

The examples from diverse groups in the chapters that follow will show how individuals have responded to this challenge, and some of their team designs.

The feedback session in the following learning task uses a set of helpful guidelines from James McCaffrey of Training Resources Group (TRG) in Washington, D.C. These are published in *Learning to Teach* (Vella, 1989, pp. 58–59), available from Save the Children in Westport, Connecticut. Participants review these simple guidelines and select the one that seems most useful to them.

TASK 17: GIVING AND GETTING FEEDBACK ON THE DESIGN AND MICROTEACHING

1.   Read the directives on feedback. Select one that would be most useful to you and tell why.

FEEDBACK

Feedback is a way of helping another person understand the impact of his or her behavior on others. It is a communication to a person (or a group) which gives that person information about how he or she affects others.

Feedback helps an individual keep his or her behavior "on target" and thus better achieve his or her goals.

Feedback is more effective when the following criteria are used:

It is specific rather than general. To be told that one is talkative will probably not be as useful as to be told that "just now when we were deciding the issue, you talked so much I stopped listening."

It is descriptive rather than judgmental. By describing one's own reaction to another's behavior, it leaves the individual free to use it or not to use it as he or she sees fit. By avoiding judgmental language, it reduces the need for the individual to respond defensively.

It takes into account the needs of both the receiver and the giver of feedback. Feedback can be destructive when it serves only our own needs and fails to consider the needs of the person on the receiving end.

It is directed toward behavior which the receiver can do something about. Frustration is only increased when a person is reminded of shortcomings over which he or she has no control.

It is solicited rather than imposed. Feedback is most useful when the receiver has formulated the kind of question which those observing can answer.

It is well-timed. In general, feedback is most useful at the earliest opportunity after the given behavior depending, of course, on the person's readiness to hear it, support available from others, etc.

It is checked to ensure clear communication. One way of doing this is to have the receiver try to rephrase the feedback in order to see if it corresponds to what the sender had in mind.

It is checked with others to ensure accuracy. Both the giver and receiver should check with others in the group as to the accuracy of the feedback. Is this one person's impression or an impression shared by others?

HELPING OTHERS GIVE FEEDBACK

Feedback from another person is one important source of data which helps tell you how your actions are affecting others. Even if you "disagree" with the feedback, it is important for you to hear it clearly and understand it.

Feedback tells you how another person sees your actions and gives you the choice of trying to change your behavior. People act on their perceptions of your actions and you may be coming across in unintended ways.

Giving someone feedback is sometimes difficult; if you keep the following in mind, you will make it easier for someone else to give you feedback that you can use.

Ask clarifying questions in order to understand the feedback.

Wait until the feedback has been given, then paraphrase the major points. Make it your goal to understand the feedback—paraphrasing and asking clarifying questions are two ways to do this.

Help the giver use the criteria for giving useful feedback. (For example, if the feedback is too general: "Could you give me a specific example of what you mean?")

Avoid making it more difficult for the giver of feedback than it already is (by reacting defensively or angrily, arguing, and so on).

Avoid explanations of "why I did that," unless asked.

Remember that feedback is one person's perceptions of your actions, not universal truth. Be active in checking out feedback with others—if two or three people give you similar feedback, there may be a pattern reflected which you might want to consider.

This simple learning task turns the TRG materials into a problem-posing handout for the active, engaged, critical perusal of the participants. There is great immediacy here, of course.

2. Questions for the team:

What did you like about your design and your teaching?

What will you change next time?

3. Questions for the participants who were your learners:

What did you like about this design?

What suggestions for changes do you offer the team?

As facilitator of such a feedback session, it is my task to keep the group on focus. It avails nothing for the team to offer excuses: "Well, we did that because we didn't have enough time." "We did that because we ran out of ink." "We included that because it is part of our company's material." I hold a very firm line here. When you are offered a suggestion for changing your design or your teaching, you say, "Thank you!" If a defensive posture is permitted to arise, the dialogue is over. This is a more demanding task for me than it appears, and I have more than once lost my reputation for sweet- ness by firmly repeating the question: What are your *suggestions* for changes? Participants so identify with their design that they are often prone to defend and protect. It is my job to keep the dialogue going and growing, knowing that the learning is in that dialogue. It is possible to offer nonjudgmental feedback.

Each teaching team gets a video of their teaching and of the feedback session. This is an immensely valuable tool that teams can use to great advantage. The videotape becomes a means of posing the problems facing each team. As one woman said, after seeing her team's performance on video, "We are all Kate Farrell!"

When teams go back to the drawing board for their second design, there is a new atmosphere of confidence and joy—laughter wells up—even as the fierceness of the struggle among the team members heats up, as it often does. This may be the high point of the week-long workshop, as teams set to incorporate all they have learned in their first design into the new one, and dig into the task of preparing a new learning needs assessment for their colleagues, designing learning tasks, making problem-posing materials, and most of all, working together effectively in dialogue.

I was once invited to a graduate school to do such a training course in three days instead of the usual five. Obviously, a great deal had to be omitted, including the second design and teaching. Never again! This popular education approach to learning is hard enough to master without inviting teachers to make bricks without straw.

By now we are on day five of the five-day training course, and everyone is duly exhausted, having worked very hard to design, teach, give and get feedback, and learn. These final tasks are review of content, review of resources available to them to continue this study of popular education, and a review of modes of evaluation. A final, summative evaluation and closure are the final tasks.

Closure

TASK 18: SYNTHESIS: POPULAR EDUCATION A TO Z

In new pairs, read over the following twenty-six questions. If you have any questions about any of them, ask. Select four you personally wish to respond to and share your response with your partner.

Inviting participants to select four of the twenty-six questions enables them to feel that they are subjects of their own learning. The dialogue between pairs proves that each participant has a cognitive grasp of much of the content. The questions, as you can see, involve reflection on experience, new skills and attitudes, as well as concepts. This task provides one checklist of competencies for the design of popular education training.

1. How do you let a learner know that she is a *subject*, not an object, in your education or training program?
2. How do you get all three circles—cognitive, affective, and psychomotor—into the design of the learning?
3. How would you do a learning needs analysis in a group of office workers?
4. How do you make tasks and materials relevant to the learners?
5. What do you perceive is meant by *engagement* as a condition of learning? What one thing can you do to engage the learners?
6. How do you use the principle of immediacy to assure accountable learning?
7. What do you do to meet resistance successfully?

8. How do you suggest one use the seven steps of planning in preparing a specific design?
9. Describe how and why you would use a critical incident.
10. Describe how and why you would use the four open questions.
11. Describe how and why you would use brainstorming.
12. What to you is the significant difference between an open and a closed question?
13. Describe how and why you would use sociodrama or role play.
14. What do you see as the essential difference between dialogue and monologue?
15. If you were to teach a lively group of adolescent boys about the danger of AIDS, how would you assure your own safety in the session?
16. How would you design the session to allow for the boys' safety so that they could learn effectively?
17. Why do you think we form objectives such as "By the end of this session all participants will have . . ."?
18. How can you discover the generative themes of a group of farmworkers?
19. Why do you use the framework for a session when you have already used the seven steps of planning? (The framework is title, warm-up, learning tasks, closure.)
20. What is your understanding of SKAs?
21. How and why would you use a web chart in a group?
22. How do you achieve inclusion among members of a group?
23. How do you as an instructor design a learning workshop that deals with both task maintenance and group maintenance?
24. Which book recommended in this workshop was most useful to you?
25. What does dialogue mean to you?
26. Why do you think respect is one of the most important principles in popular education?

This task establishes a confirmed confidence in the group. They are beginning to know that they know, by virtue of their two designs, their teaching practice, and their control of the concepts.

As the five-day workshop concludes, resources in popular education are examined; participants are invited to contribute names and telephone numbers of people who can help develop desired skills; and coalitions and communities of scholars for further action research are identified and set up if necessary.

TASK 19: NEXT STEPS

Look at the attached list of resources for ongoing study and action research on popular education. What would you suggest we add? What are your questions?

The list of resources is determined by the context of the course, but it will include international publishers like WomenInk of New York, coalitions such as the North American Alliance of Popular Educators, and educational resources such as the Center for International Education at the University of Massachusetts, Amherst. The items included merely prime the pump for participants to add groups and resources they have used in their particular discipline or context. The list grows as learners recognize that they have resources available to them for ongoing study. Jubilee Popular Education Center is one of those resources, with training offered three times a year, as well as fellowship programs, a second course, which is a follow-up of this training course, and Master Trainers' classes, which prepare men and women to teach others how to do popular education.

Before being invited to evaluate this course, participants are asked to review the differences between immediate and long-term or longitudinal evaluation indicators, and between qualitative and quantitative indicators.

TASK 20: EVALUATION INDICATORS

1. Read the following short summary of evaluation indicators:

Evaluation indicators of skills, knowledge, and attitudes learned during an educational event can be immediate or longitudinal. Immediate indicators are present changes in behavior that manifest new concepts, skills, and attitudes. Longitudinal indicators are behaviors that manifest themselves over time. For example, you have used the seven steps of planning in your designs; you have included warm-ups and inclusion in your dialogue about the designs; and you have affirmed one another as colleagues in the feedback session. These are present behaviors, immediate indicators of learning.

Evaluation indicators can be quantitative and qualitative. Quantitative indicators are measurable in numerical units; qualitative indicators are measurable in affective units. For example, you designed twice, you led two different warm-up tasks, and you read one book. These are quantitative indicators. You are excited enough about popular education to ask for a list of publications beyond what is in the bibliography. You designed the second design with much more confidence. You questioned and argued with the instructor about meanings and applications. These are qualitative indicators.

INDICATORS FOR EVALUATION OF LEARNING

2. At your table, identify one immediate indicator of learning from this course for you personally. Identify one longitudinal indicator of learning you can anticipate will be in place for you in six months. We'll share a sample of your evaluation indicators.

3. Consider the following scenario:

You met Kate Farrell after she had completed this course in popular education. You saw her in action in Kentucky where she made visits to each mother's home before beginning her course, doing a learning needs assessment and getting to meet the mothers. In her training session with them, Kate called all the mothers and their children by name, and they did the same for one another. This was a qualitative indicator. She prepared three learning tasks for the mothers, bringing in real food for them to use. She found that fewer mothers dropped out of the course this time around. These were quantitative indicators for her. What other indicators might she find?

4. What differences do you see between qualitative and quantitative indicators?

The evaluation of the entire course is done after a review of the achievement-based objectives, their expectations named on day one, and the content. Ideally, evaluation reveals that the instructors have indeed done what they contracted to do, that the design has been accountable, and that instructors and participants have been accountable to one another. Participants are asked to take time to write down these evaluations. It is a learning task!

TASK 21: EVALUATION AND CLOSURE

1. Review the achievement-based objectives and the content of the training workshop. Review this chart with your expectations. What strikes you?
2. Please respond to the following subjective evaluation questions:

What was most useful to you ?

How do you see yourself using what you learned here this week?

Who else do you know who might be interested in doing such a workshop?

What suggestions do you offer for changes in the program, logistics, and/or process?

3. Who do you specifically wish to thank for what you have learned here this week?

The closing ceremony is a small ritual to celebrate the learning that has taken place, honoring the service individuals offered to one another and all that took place to make the training program work. Such an opportunity for personal thanks raises energy and shows participants once again how they are resources to one another. They each receive a certificate celebrating their achievement.

What I have described in this chapter is the generic training course for teaching skills, knowledge, and attitudes to those who wish to use popular education in their own teaching of other teachers. Obviously this is a work in progress. It has never been done the same way twice, yet it is somehow always the same. In the next six chapters, I will describe highlights of the implementation of this design in six very diverse situations: with health professionals in Chile, with AIDS prevention teams in Haiti, with Literacy Volunteers of America, with a veterans' affairs hospital staff working with substance abusers, with a rural Arkansas community development bank, and with leaders and trainers from nonprofit groups in New England.

3

Group Size and the Role of the "Professor"

Training Trainers in Community Health

> Problem-posing education bases itself on creativity and stimulates true reflection and action upon reality, thereby responding to the vocation of persons as beings in formation.
> —Paulo Freire (1993, p. 64)

Many lessons were learned from a popular education training course done with health professionals in Chile. Two of these lessons will be highlighted in this chapter: first, the principle of *scale*—that the size of the group directly affects the level of learning—and second, the *role of the instructor*—you will see how useful it was for the instructor to take a quiet role. This case also shows how to deal with *resistance* by fidelity to the design. As you read this example, you will be invited in the sections entitled "Your Turn" to apply to this situation the principles presented in the first two chapters, and to suggest alternative approaches.

Preparation

Joaquin Montero is the head of internal medicine and professor of community medicine at the hospital of the Pontifical Catholic University of Chile in Santiago. He spent two years at the University of North Carolina (UNC), Chapel Hill, and at the University of New Mexico's medical school exploring his dream of designing a special course for teams of primary care specialists who would work in rural Chile and those urban pockets that were neglected by traditional medical resources.

Montero studied popular education while he was working on his master's degree in public health at UNC's School of Public Health. He was delighted to have found a course that actually showed him what to do and how to do it to fulfill his dream of accessible community health education. He invited me to Chile to work with the young physicians and other health professionals he was teaching at Universidad Católica. The university had funds from the Kellogg Foundation and World Health Organization to develop a course in community-based internal medicine. The health professionals—doctors, nurses, and social workers—would in turn be teaching local health educators, midwives, and health workers. Montero felt that these professionals needed to learn an approach to adult education different from what they had experienced in their own professional training.

Rodrigo Escalona is a Chilean psychiatrist whose studies at Duke University's School of Medicine were nearing completion when I received Montero's invitation to do a train-the-trainer course in Santiago. I emphatically set conditions on the language of the course: it would be done in Spanish by first-language Spanish speakers. I had had enough experience with "experts" coming onto the international scene and teaching local professionals in English as if that were the language of the gods. Montero agreed and invited Escalona to be the leader of the course. Rosa Walker, a physician who worked with Montero in Santiago, had also been a student of popular education at UNC's School of Public Health. She and a North American Jubilee Fellow, Ellen Turgasen, who had experience as a nurse in Peru, worked long and hard together to translate the generic course presented in Chapter Two and all the materials needed into Spanish, and to adapt the program for this particular Chilean context.

Montero and I spent hours communicating by fax and phone to set up the program. He wanted forty health professionals from his new university program to do the course. I insisted on a maximum of twenty and agreed to do the course twice over a period of two or three weeks. As a result of this experience, I now know that the number of participants should be capped at twelve, not twenty, and that we might have worked best over a period of five weeks! In attempting to develop skills, knowledge, and attitudes for popular education approaches with twenty adults in five days, I gave these health professionals a false message. This is a practical course, needing time for mentored practice in design and facilitation. In five days there was simply not enough time to give twenty learners the guided practice they needed to confirm these new skills. Then, since this is the way they learned about popular education, they could be expected to do the same with twenty village health workers, and end up wondering why their courses were not effective.

The variable of *scale* is now a vital consideration for me. Scale involves both the time frame and the number of students. In this Chilean example, not enough attention was given to the scale of the effort. I hope the health professionals who participated in that course read this book to see this confession and to learn what my research has proven: less is more.

Escalona saw no problem in setting the tasks and leading the training. I would be there as his silent partner, my ancient and rusty Spanish straining to be unleashed. Escalona had read the translated course materials and a few books in English on the popular education approach, including my *Learning to Teach* (1989). Initially he was not very impressed. In light of his studies in psychiatry, this all appeared to him to be a lightweight discipline. As he led the course, it became apparent how surprised he was by what was happening. The consequent transformation of his beliefs about adult education led to the event at the Veterans' Affairs Medical Center described in Chapter Seven.

Many of the Chilean participants prepared for the course by reading some of the books in English and Spanish that were listed in the course's bibliography. The content and process of this participative, problem-posing, accountable approach to adult education were not entirely foreign to them, since they had already been exposed to it in Montero's classes at the university. Chile was, after all, where Paulo Freire had done his original research for his seminal work *Pedagogy of the Oppressed* (1993). In a planning meeting before the course began, I had the chance to review with the team the list of participants. The program was examined in light of the specific needs of the group, who were coming to the course largely out of respect for Joaquin Montero. None of these health professionals could be said to have a felt need to teach more effectively. I could feel their curiosity about the length of the course because they expected me to talk at them the whole time. I could also feel some impatience: Why would it take five days to learn about community education? I speak of how we dealt with this unconscious resistance later in this chapter.

The Design

The course was opened at the medical school of the Pontifical Catholic University of Chile as the first activity of the new primary care/internal medicine residency program, with formal speeches by the minister of health and the dean of the medical school, and by Montero as head of the department of internal medicine. The opening was televised nationally. This was clearly seen as an important event.

When the participants opened their course books they found a short quote from Paulo Freire's *Pedagogy of the Oppressed* (1993) on the first page. It summarized the purpose of the venture: "No one teaches another, nor is anyone self-taught. People teach each other mediated by the world. . ." (Freire, 1993, p. 61). The subtitle of the course book was also telling: *Tecnicas para ensenar a aprender en el trabajo y la Salud*, that is, ways of teaching in order to learn in work and health. The course itself was subtitled *Seminario intensivo sobre diseno y practica de la ensenanza no tradicional de adultos*, that is, an intensive seminar about the design and practice of nontraditional teaching of adults.

All of this should have warned the twenty participants in the first course that something unusual was afoot. They found themselves at a training center in a peculiar classroom with five tables set up for four men and women at each table, with a name card in front of each person's place. They were seated facing one another. Where was the professor? Who had stolen the podium? When would the learned lectures start?

The strangeness continued with the first learning task set by Escalona after a short welcome by Montero. It was a warm-up: select an object that symbolizes your work. Say what? These were overworked, busy professionals, reasonably impressed by their place in the world of medicine in Chile. They had already graduated from medical, social work, and nursing schools and had demanding jobs in community medicine. They expected a series of learned lectures about adult education, and here they were being asked to talk about symbols of their work. It was shocking, to say the least.

They cooperated, however, humoring the international consultant, who on this first day was still called Dr. Vella, and their colleague, the Chilean psychiatrist. Their reluctance dissipated as they listened to one another at their tables, meeting colleagues for the first time at a new level of symbol and connotative description. I could see the found objects they selected: their beepers, their white coats, their stethoscopes. Some ventured to select their keys or a leaf from the trees outside. I heard the tone of dialogue at the table grow more animated and the laughter increase. Escalona synthesized the first task competently and welcomed them to the week of hard work "para ensenar a aprender"—learning how to teach in order to learn.

When they were asked for their expectations in the second task, after a review of the objectives and the topical program, they were evidently nonplussed. It was a first for them, to be asked, What do you expect to learn this week? Again, they entered into the task, doing it in pairs and taking energy from one another. Their expectations, written one per blank card, were indicative of their interests:

How can we reach illiterate village women?

How can we teach them what they need to know?

How can we work together more effectively?

Why participation?

How can we motivate learners?

How can we forget what we learned about teaching in
medical school?

What's the history of this problem-posing approach?

The latter was an interesting question to me since Paulo Freire
had written *Pedagogy of the Oppressed* in Chile while working on a
national literacy campaign for the Frei government. Although
Chile had recently had an election, the military power was omni-
present and Freire's name was not used without caution. I realized
it had taken courage for the Chilean team to put the excerpt from
Freire's book on the front of the learning materials for the course.
We would have to steer carefully through the political concerns of
the participants. Can you see why it was vital that the steering committee be composed of nationals? I did not even have a consultative
voice in this regard. I would be leaving in a fortnight. The participants would be staying and would be held accountable for their
educational approach. Few of them, young as they were, had been
able to read any of Freire's books, which had been outlawed for
years in Chile.

Escalona was able to connect their expectations to the achievement-based objectives of the course. He explained that the design
of the course would be informed by these expectations as far as possible in that they would be used by the group along with the objectives as a guide for formative evaluation each evening and as the
basis of the summative, final evaluation on the fifth day.

YOUR TURN

Since needs assessment has been proven to be such a vital
aspect of this approach to adult learning, what would you

suggest could have been done to set up a dialogue around the participants' felt needs and the objectives of the course before the first day? For example, the steering committee might have had them fax a response to a set of survey questions in Spanish, or had them name their expectations when they registered for the course. What else?

As the small groups worked on learning task after task at their tables, the tone of their dialogue rose in vigor. Escalona proved to be a competent facilitator who quickly learned how to echo what he heard learners say and how to synthesize a dialogue. Each participant had among their materials a set of cards containing the fifty principles and practices of popular education in Spanish. I posted these cards on a chart as we used each principle or practice. The participants were surprised at noon of the first day to discover how many of the principles and practices they had already used. These simple materials serve as useful mnemonics.

Dealing with Resistance

In the afternoon of the first day when we performed the task of formative evaluation using the force field analysis (Task Eleven in Chapter Two)—What was most useful? What changes would you suggest?—one physician commented that he really wanted to hear from Dr. Vella! He had not come to talk to his peers, he complained, and he suggested that I be more active on the second day. We welcomed his comments and did not defend the design or explain why I was so silent a partner. Such resistance is not diminished by arguing. On the fifth day of the course, the same doctor apologized to the group for what he had said on that first day. He humbly confessed, "I just did not know how much there was to learn from all of you."

We, the workshop leaders, noticed that the style of the participants' dress changed as the week progressed. The men went from formal suits, vests, and ties on day one to khakis and comfortable sport shirts on day five. Such an unscheduled change in uniform is a delicate indicator of a change in attitude which the instructor of a popular education workshop can silently celebrate.

Roles and Tasks

Each learning task was written in Spanish on a chart that was posted for all to see. Escalona set the tasks, and the groups, which were new each day, worked assiduously at them in the time frame he set. He then invited responses from the table groups, where the actual learning was taking place. At times I would add my comments in English and Escalona would translate them for those few who did not understand. I was not a passive resource person, waiting to be called upon. I entered the dialogue when I felt I had something valuable to offer.

The participants loved the case study of Kate Farrell (Task 8), who became, in Spanish, Eliana Ferrer. Everyone agreed that there was no hyperbole in this story. They said it was exactly what was happening that very day in any rural Chilean setting.

Escalona gave an outstanding performance in his illustration of monologue (Task 9). Perhaps his recent experience in medical school had prepared him for this. In any case, the participants responded with alacrity to this learning task. Their concern was the classic one: How do we teach what we know people need to know without using the banking approach or monologue?

We invited them to be patient, assuring them that they would discover a response to that question before long. In fact, they all finally gave themselves the response to that query in their small groups, as they struggled with their designs and microteaching.

The second day was replete with substantive theory, which was taught through the participative, problem-posing, accountable process they were learning. The chart of cards of principles and practices was growing! Escalona explained each principle and practice as participants requested clarification, and when he was not sure, I explained in English and he translated. My role was still that of second fiddle: present, observing, sitting still, paying attention, usually keeping quiet until asked to speak.

On the third day the opening task was a warm-up involving the design of a synthesis song by each small group. The Latin musical talent in the group came to the surface. It was touching to see these busy health professionals laughing and singing together to capture all they had learned in the first two days.

There were two sample designs in their materials. One was a design, translated into Spanish, prepared by a graduate student of public health who was working with Mexican migrant workers in an agricultural hamlet of North Carolina. The Chilean participants were impressed by her development of the participative design. The title of the other design was, in Spanish, *"Tenemos que cambiar estas reuniones."* Perhaps the translation lost the innuendo of the English title: "We've got to stop meeting like this!" (see the sample design provided in Task 14 in Chapter Two). All the elements of a design were there for them to examine, to learn from, and to critique. The learning tasks around each of these sample designs were What are your questions? and What would you change in this design?

After examining the two sample designs, the participants set up ten design teams of two people each and worked assiduously using the seven steps of planning and the fifty Spanish cards containing the principles and practices. They all selected content connected with their clinical efforts in their communities, since the adult learners in this exercise would be their peers in this group of health professionals. With each group teaching for one hour, there was a great opportunity to learn from one another. The ongoing feedback to each group proved useful to everyone. After all ten teams had taken their turn teaching, each team went back to the drawing board to design again, using all they had learned from the feedback sessions. Each teaching team first evaluated their own work, responding to the questions: What did you like about your design and teaching? What will you change next time? Then their peers, whom they had been teaching, gave them feedback using similar questions: What did you like about their design and teaching? What suggestions do you have for changes?

Here was a case in which safety in the structure of the learning task was imperative. These men and women were peers in a highly competitive profession. They had to feel safe in order to give and receive this feedback. We pointed out that all feedback was offered as a suggestion, in a consultative voice, so presenters did not have to defend their designs or their teaching.

This approach to feedback prevents the development of antagonistic relationships in the group. Those who offer suggestions to the presenters are expected to do so with a consultative voice as allies and friends. The presenters are the ones who decide what part of the feedback they can actually use in their next design. There is no place here for a defensive reply. This is an ingenious way of bringing dialogue into the feedback process.

Montero was not able to be present for the whole week. He did hear rumblings of delight, however, from the participants, and was present on day five to celebrate the end of the event. We arranged to have another ceremony on the last day of the second session, with everyone who had taken part in both week-long courses. Some of the participants traveled hours from their rural stations to be present for that one-hour ceremony, bringing friends with them to meet their new colleagues and to celebrate their new learning.

The health professionals who participated in these sessions set up a rural health coalition that held monthly meetings to do further study of the principles and practices of popular education and to examine their teaching designs. When I expressed concern that the group might easily become exclusive, with typical Chilean adroitness they all agreed to each bring along to each meeting one other person who might be interested in participative adult learning. This meant that their study group would honor the principle of inclusion they had just learned. One young physician brought along his fiancée, a health professional who wanted to share what he had just learned.

In the written evaluations of the first week many participants said they appreciated the fact that I, the "professor," could sit silently and listen to the Spanish dialogue. I liked that, too, and want to go on record for this achievement to astound my incredulous family and friends! I learned that I can sit still, be quiet, and pay attention.

Freire's provocative comment that only the student can name the moment of the death of the professor, sets up a difficult responsibility. Rare are the students with that kind of courage; rarer still are the professors who willingly self-destruct as "professor." Yet we see in this instance that my silence was a most useful factor in the participants' learning, and a vital part of the model I had come to Chile to teach. This is indeed a new role for the professor.

The Second Session

The team of instructors had learned a few important things from the first session that we were able then to use in the second week. We moved to a brighter room, with more space for tables. We included a handout on axioms in Spanish. The dean emeritus of the school of medicine was present in the second week. He was about to open a training center for community health workers and found this training course timely.

When I was attempting to explain what I meant by the axiom, "Don't tell what you can ask; don't ask if you know the answer; tell, in dialogue," I explained by saying, "My middle name is Catherine. I would not ask, What is my middle name, since I know the answer, but I could engage you all by telling, in dialogue, My middle name is Catherine. It is my mother's name. Who else here has a Catherine in their life?" The dean answered, "My first granddaughter who was born yesterday morning." The power of dialogue! We became friends there and then, celebrating our respective Catherines.

The asking spoken of in that axiom is not testing. We have all experienced the constant testing that goes on in the traditional education system. The testing of adult learners prevails. The popular education approach insists that testing is not teaching. Being tested is not learning. I would go so far as to maintain that testing is often antithetical to effective adult learning.

The second session group had heard all the excited responses of their colleagues and peers from the first group, so there was much less resistance in the early days of this five-day course. The instructors were more at ease, too, aware that the process worked in spite of language differences. Rosa Walker took over from Escalona. It was useful for all to see that the process of leading the learning tasks had a life of its own and was not dependent upon the person. The operator factor, in this case, was not primary.

In the second session, some of the more ambiguous translations that had been questioned in the first week were changed. All of this learning argued in favor of an improved second week of course work and materials! This was indeed praxis: do it, examine it, reflect on what happened, and change. In any case, I have learned that it is not effective to work with twenty participants in this course, as was done in Santiago. It is imperative to limit the size of the group in a training course to twelve participants in order to give more time to the learning needs of each individual.

The microteaching in each of the two weeks was exciting, full of humor and activity. In the second week, one of the design groups was from the school of education. I had urged the two men to work with others in their design and microteaching, but they said, "No, we want to work together because we know how to do this." Their microteaching was entirely didactic, with hardly any evidence of the principles and practices of popular education. Their colleagues gave them strong feedback, suggesting that they revise their approach. It was for me a good example of cultural resistance to changing habits that die hard. The most difficult set of learners are those who are sure they have nothing to learn.

How did we adapt the generic model to the Chilean situation? The adaptation was not only in the translation but also in the constant references to medical, clinical, and community health issues that honored the context of the participating health professionals. The generic model presented in Chapter Two was so changed in Chile as to be unrecognizable at times. That is as it should be. The model is never used as a recipe.

What were the lessons learned from the Chilean experience? As I've already said, I personally learned that the adapted model works without dependence on the operator factor, and that you cannot work with twenty people, since they do not have adequate time to reflect and to respond, nor to design and practice. Somehow, the economic issues pertinent to these scale needs must be organized so that groups can be limited to twelve participants. The workshop planners learned the value of meeting resistance with equanimity and utter faith in the design. If we had argued with the young doctor who wanted to hear "the professor," he might have left the workshop. We learned the value of sitting still, keeping quiet, and paying attention, a new role for the professor.

I learned the value of the coalition that was formed on that last day. Twelve months after the first courses, Rosa Walker and a nurse colleague, Soledad Riviera, offered a follow-up course for all participants. Montero has plans to do such courses with new health professionals in the future. The coalition participants support one another at meetings by sharing their efforts to use this problem-posing, participative, popular education approach. They recognize this as an important research agenda.

The introductory course to popular education for the training of trainers has a long way to go before it becomes fully accessible to busy doctors and nurses. The present generic course needs years of praxis to shape it into a sound, accessible curriculum. The experience in Chile was and continues to be an important laboratory for training health professionals in the skills of popular education.

Montero told me the following story. One of the doctors who had completed the course was invited later in the year to give a paper on his work in the rural community at a very important national conference of Chilean physicians held at the medical school of the Pontifical Catholic University. He invited a village health worker, an unlettered, wise, competent woman, to speak to the conference while he stood by. She did so, to a standing ovation from the gathered physicians. Such an event is a cogent indicator of the power of popular education to evoke creative expressions of respect for the adult learner.

YOUR TURN

A new master trainer program at Jubilee has prepared men and women, some of whom are competent in Spanish, to be leaders of the training course. The Spanish-speaking master trainers will be going to Chile to work with a group of thirty health professionals in three week-long workshops. What is your advice to them, in light of what you have just read about this first effort? How can they learn the culture of the people they will be teaching? How can they best use the original cadre of popular educators from the health community? How should they relate to the existing coalition? What other questions would you ask them? What advice would you give them?

4

The Importance
of Dialogue

Training in Nonprofit Organizations

Because liberating action is dialogical in nature, dialogue cannot be a posteriori to that action, but must be concomitant with it. And since liberation must be a permanent condition, dialogue becomes a continuing aspect of liberating action.
—Paulo Freire (1993, p. 120)

Working with trainers and directors of nonprofit groups in New England has taught me a great deal about the process of training trainers in popular education methods. Again, busy, overworked individuals find it difficult to stop long enough to examine their process of community education, to share their experience, and to consider alternatives. At the end of a week-long program, the hardworking director of a Boston project lamented that he had waited so long for this kind of experience. "It has changed not only my approach to this work, but my approach to living."

The hardest part of working with this energetic group of activists was to channel their energy, to invite them to reflect before they decide what to teach and what their objectives are (they dash to the how), and to agree that, in fact, less is more (they invariably want to teach too much in too short a time). There is sometimes in such groups the individual who simply does not fit into the value system or common structures of the group. The case described in this chapter was a lesson in how to deal with this person with respect and inclusion as well as with tough love.

Preparation

Richard Schramm is a dynamic, quiet-spoken professor of political science. When he was at Tufts University, he conceived and founded the Management and Community Development Institute (MCDI), a five-day intensive summer institute held at Tufts with a menu of courses for managers, administrators, community organizers, educators and trainers, fundraisers, and boards of nonprofit groups. He wanted to teach these folks, in a short time and on a low budget, how to organize and manage their nonprofit groups with top-of-the-line skills. In 1989, he invited the staff of Jubilee Popular Education Center to do a three-hour workshop on community education for a small group of nonprofit trainers, community educators, and administrators. Schramm himself completed the course in 1990, which had grown into a one-day session. Participants clamored for more time to learn and practice the concepts, skills, and attitudes presented in the session, so the next year a two-day course was held during the five-day institute. Jubilee now does a three-day course for the MCDI, with two tracks to allow for twenty-four participants. I am working toward expanding this to five days. Last year, people came to the MCDI from all over the United States and Canada. During the six years that this short training course has been offered, it has changed drastically. Jubilee has learned a great deal, and the nonprofit groups have become more sophisticated and demanding, thanks to the success of the MCDI and their own efforts at professionalism.

The Nonprofit Education and Training Program (NET) is funded by the Kellogg Foundation. The MCDI is one of the programs offered by NET. It offers the five-day training course to nonprofit groups throughout New England at a reduced cost, and the second course for nonprofit participants who have completed the basic course. This chapter offers highlights from these two courses, illustrating how the skills, attitudes, and knowledge of popular education are relevant to nonprofit groups.

Recruiting and selection of nonprofit participants is done by NET staff. They register twelve participants, send them the draft course outline, and tell them to expect to hear from Jubilee. Once Jubilee staff get names, affiliations, and telephone numbers from NET, we start the needs assessment, spending time on the phone with a sample of the twelve participants, inquiring about their role and task in their nonprofit group, their expectations of the program, and their potential application of the training skills they will learn.

This learning needs assessment does two things. First, it offers a model of the use of a learning needs assessment, in this case, a telephone survey. Second, it provides a sense of who is coming, the profile of the group, the types of people and their involvement in the community. As I often say, the learning needs assessment does not form the program, but it drastically *informs* it.

Once, in preparing for a second course with NET, Jubilee staff did a telephone survey of six of the twelve participants. One of the persons whom we had not included in the sample came to the course without having done any preparation for the course. He had hurriedly read the course outline, probably distracted by his many responsibilities. When the course started, he discovered he had to leave because of an emergency. This incident offers an example of a possible third function of the learning needs assessment: to remind participants of the requirements for the course.

The Design

The NET course participants come from very busy work sites. It is common knowledge that many nonprofit groups are understaffed and underfunded. While they are grateful for the opportunity for specialized training, and while they have no doubt heard good things about the course from colleagues and peers who have taken it at the MCDI summer session or at another time through NET, they are reluctant to give up a week of their busy lives for the session. They are activists who spend their days and nights doing more than their job descriptions require. The course must start out with vigor to assure them that their time will be well spent.

It has been the pattern to start the NET course on a late afternoon prior to the first day. This allows time for setting the stage and for inviting participants to review the program and name their own personal expectations. These first two hours consist of the initial warm-up, introductions, and inviting people to talk about their organizations and their achievements. This latter activity is called "brag time." Since people are arranged at tables with others they have only just met, and because the time frame for the task is short, they are willing to talk about their work. The timing here is important. Jubilee recommends allowing the groups enough time to do this task at a brisk pace, because the shorter the time, the higher the energy to do a learning task. Set time limits clearly. Keep to them. If people have not completed their sharing, they will let you know. Once the small-group sharing is completed, sharing moves to the level of the large group, with the instructor providing encouragement and affirmation. In this way, the instructor provides a good example of the role of the instructor in the popular education approach: setting tasks; inviting sharing; echoing, affirming, and encouraging participants; and synthesizing responses. In a setting in which the instructor plays such a role, the participants can be excited by their peers, and find themselves learning from one another. They know they will learn more from one another as the week progresses. No one has more authority than a peer.

Next, the objectives, content, and topical program are reviewed, with emphasis on the expectation that participants will prepare an actual design for training to take home for immediate use. As they share expectations, they share the energy they have for their work and for the course. A preview of day two is necessary at this time to make sure they know what to expect. At the end of this first two-hour session, trainers and community educators generally leave excited and hopeful. This is one example of the principle of immediacy in action.

On day two, new small groups are formed. The generic program is followed, making amendments in context and content to reflect the participants' situations in nonprofit groups. Task 4 still presents

Kate Farrell as a nurse in Appalachia, since that is far enough away from their situation to be safe and close enough (many of them *are* Kate Farrell!) to be immediate. As far as possible, with this group, use of educational jargon is avoided, with cues taken from their own use of language.

On day three, as participants begin to form teams for design and teaching, there is often resistance and reluctance to get on with the task. It is often difficult to assure this group that they will be safe in the venture of design and practice teaching. In one session, the instructors felt like they had hit a thick brick wall and there was no going around it. The teams were so deeply resistant to the learning task of designing a short program and teaching it to the others that I simply called for an early lunch, and let them work it out among themselves. When they returned in the afternoon, there was evidence that they had done some significant soul searching and were ready to try the challenging task. It is the job of the instructors to make the situation as safe as possible without taking away the challenge.

Before the participants begin to use the seven steps of planning to design their practice teaching, and to support participants' choice of content to teach, the instructors provide a list of possible themes that they have heard from each individual throughout the week relating to their nonprofit organizations, their professional interests, or their family situations. A hospice trainer, for example, talked a lot about the universal precautions against the spread of HIV and AIDS. A new mother talked about the issue of child care. A youth worker was a newly licensed pilot. A community organizer in housing clearly knew a great deal about rent control legislation. Once the question of what they will teach has been reasonably answered, the teams settle down to the actual task of design.

Working in design teams is a challenge, especially for individuals who work in diverse nonprofit groups. They live and work in teams, and this workshop effort is quite intentional practice for them. We urge teams to reflect on the bicycle model (see Figure 2.3) used to describe task and group maintenance and to use it in their small design group. In this NET course, the teamwork is always vigorous and noisy with lots of laughter. One team worked on a design for teaching the group how to prepare a funding proposal; another designed a half-hour session on appropriate physical exercise for people over forty! The diversity of designs reflected the diversity within the group.

As teams design, their attention is drawn by the instructors to two consistent problems. First, they are cautioned, don't rush to the "how" (learning tasks and materials)—that is, use all the seven steps of planning before deciding what learning tasks to set. For some inexplicable reason, participants from nonprofit organizations tend to move directly into the "how" without adequate reflection on who they are teaching, why they are doing it, the time frame and the site, and their content and objectives. The second caution is parallel: do not have too much "what" (content) for your "when" (time frame):—that is, do not try to teach more than the time frame allows. In the NET events, teams teach for forty minutes or so and then get and give feedback. Virtually all teams suffer from chronic "too much what for their when," despite the warnings. They have a sense that more is more. Experience suggests, on the contrary, that less is more.

YOUR TURN

How can instructors in a training course in popular education both support the design teams with a standard structure and also challenge them to stretch their skills and create a daring design? How can instructors best be resource people without intruding on participants' creativity, while offering suggestions to enable them to avoid the usual sand traps of discouragement and disagreement?

Dealing with a Troubled Participant

One NET course included an individual who was indeed troubled. He managed to oppose everything that was being done or suggested, he clamored for attention in large-group dialogue, and he monopolized the conversation at his table group. This behavior became evident on day two of the five-day workshop. What to do? The principles of inclusion and respect apply here, as well as safety for the entire group. This experience was not new for me, as I had met this type of individual at other training events. I called a break, and while participants moved to get cups of coffee, I invited the troubled gentleman to walk with me outside the training room. In a kindly dialogue, I confronted him with his behavior and asked what he felt was the matter. What could we do to meet his needs? In this case, the young man was startled: "Who, me?" He assured me he was content with the course, and went back to his small group with assurances to me that he would be a better listener. He was.

In some cases, this confrontation works; in others, it does not. It may be necessary to invite a person to consider leaving the workshop. I did that once, and the woman involved agreed wholeheartedly with me. She wanted a way out. The most important aspect of dealing with individuals with specific problems is to deal with them immediately. In a five-day workshop, the problem will only grow worse. It is the instructor's job to protect the learning of the larger group while respecting and listening to the needs of the troubled participant.

The Emergence of Leadership

Leadership emerges within the group of participants. People early on recognize those with whom they wish to form a design team on day three; they readily acknowledge the authority of those who have been in the field for many years. A twenty-two-year-old woman from a tenant housing organization in a small New England town spoke with such authority as to belie her years. Everyone listened. There is no need for the instructor to do more than affirm such strength. Individuals and teams in these groups take care of one another. It is a professional trait, born of years of experience. Group maintenance is often sensitive and comprehensive. The

instructor's role and task is to recognize and celebrate that maintenance when it occurs, but not to overstep.

Can you see how the context and the nature of the group
always shape the training course? The health professionals in Chile
used the same learning tasks as these New England nonprofit
leaders, but the tasks and outcomes were significantly different. The
difference is in the context, not in the content.

Within the design teams, leadership also emerges, reflecting
what has happened in the course so far. When I, as instructor, have
been listening sensitively to the group throughout and have worked
hard to keep their energy up, I see the teams doing the same for one
another. We teach the way we have been taught.

Nonprofit groups work in a tough political environment. They continually work to support themselves through fundraising, they are
responsible to boards of directors who themselves need thorough
training, and they often work against the political current in a climate of opposition. They need training in effective group maintenance and task maintenance. They are doers who need to learn
complex theories of management and political organization by the
most active means. This approach to adult learning with all its principles and practices fits them like a glove. They enjoy the popular
education training course, and find what they learn there to be
effective in their work both within their own nonprofit organizations and in their communities.

A woman who single-handedly runs an organization that
recruits and trains volunteers to teach English to refugees, mostly
from Southeast Asia, shared her feeling of new strength. "I now
know how to organize the volunteer training using the seven steps
of planning. I have a checklist of the principles and practices to
assure myself that I am teaching accountably during the volunteer
training, and I can offer this same checklist to the volunteer teachers
who work one-on-one with refugee families. We can together

constantly ask, How do they know they know? as we evaluate our programs."

The five-day course, and the second course need to be refined again and again to fit the participant groups more effectively. Any academic, abstract language or activity falls short with them and must be amended. No other set of adult learners has so challenged the popular education approach. It is a very healthy situation. Since the demands of their organizations are so great, their need for follow-up and support is also great. They have formed a cluster group who meet regularly in Boston to examine their use of the principles and practices and to share designs. This group corresponds to the rural health coalition working in Chile. An evaluation team is presently at work through NET to examine what difference the training course and the second course have made in the staff orientations, board training, community meetings, and neighborhood organizing done by these nonprofit groups. These men and women in the New England area are a stimulating laboratory for examining problem-posing, participative, popular education approaches to adult learning.

5

Honoring the Role of the Learner

Training with Health Professionals

> If true commitment to the people, involving the transformation
> of the reality by which they are oppressed, requires a theory of
> transforming action, this theory cannot fail to assign the people
> a fundamental role in the transformation process.
> —Paulo Freire (1993, p. 107)

The danger of the spread of HIV and AIDS throughout the island nation of Haiti has recently risen to explosive levels. Save the Children, an international community development program, organized a coalition of sister agencies to plan together and to teach Haitian farmers in the Central Plateau how to avoid this encroaching plague. The members of the coalition were doctors, nurses, social workers, and administrators of health organizations and clinics in the area.

Thanks to the funding agencies U.S. AID and the World Health Organization, Save the Children had a good grasp of current epidemiological research. What they did not know was how to teach community groups with accountability when the issue was a matter of life and death. A training course program run by Jubilee was held in March 1994 during a politically volatile period. It offered many lessons on the training process itself, including how to organize and respect subgroups within the larger group, how the Haitian context shaped the training program, and how emerging leadership in a coalition affects the training program of that group.

Preparation

The seven steps of planning were used to organize the training course.

Who? In the face of the Save the Children organizers' request to work with forty or fifty members of the coalition, Jubilee insisted on fewer than twenty participants. The number was finally brought down to eighteen. The participants included physicians, nurses, and social workers. Most of them were Haitian, some trained in Haiti and some in the United States. They were a courageous group, working in the mountainous Central Plateau of a nation that has a long history of violence. Any one of them could have found a safe spot elsewhere in the world in which to use their professional skills and knowledge. They knew where they wanted to be and what they wanted to do.

Why? The situation in Haiti was growing more and more out of control. The number of AIDS cases had increased exponentially in recent years. People come back to their family homes in the plateau to die after becoming infected with the virus in the port city. These health professionals were desperate for an accountable form of adult education that could be used in communities to discourage young people from going to the city in the first place and from participating in activities that lead to AIDS.

When? The participants agreed to a five-day course in which they could design programs for training village and community health professionals who would in turn teach their neighbors.

Where? A church center in the Central Plateau offered an inexpensive, accessible location where everyone could live for one week.

What? The content was not very different from that of the generic course that you read about in Chapter Two, except that it, like the objectives, was set in terms relating directly to AIDS education training:

How adults learn (Knowles) as this applies to preparing
    health professionals to teach community groups about
    HIV and AIDS

Lewin's dozen principles for learning as they apply to community learning about HIV and AIDS

The advantage of the problem-posing approach, of dialogue over monologue in teaching people about AIDS

Achievement-based objectives for community training

Principles and practices of popular education as these enhance training skills of community health educators

Uses of warm-ups

Cognitive, affective, and psychomotor aspects of learning that are necessary in teaching about AIDS

How to do a learning needs assessment in a community and with health educators

Generative themes of a community or of a training group

How groups work

The seven steps of planning to design effective community education

Design of problem-posing learning materials

How to ask open questions

How to get and give feedback

Evaluation of learning through immediate and long-term indicators

The learner as subject and decision maker

Techniques for participative adult learning: case studies, found objects, music, dance, sociodrama, effective charts, pictures, videos, brainstorming, snow cards

The participants in this program needed to learn all of these skills, knowledge, and attitudes so that they could teach the popular education approach to their local health educators, the leaders of the coalition organizations. Often these participants would not be doing the community education themselves, but would be training their staff how to do it effectively.

YOUR TURN

How much of the theory of adult learning do you think is
needed to move these AIDS activists to teach differently?
How about simply inviting them to work with newly framed
materials that demand a dialogical approach? This would cut
down the time they spend in training. How would it enable
them to then teach others to use dialogue? These are tough
questions not specific to this AIDS education training.
You will often be asked to take a shortcut: to teach people to
use new materials without considering the theoretical base.
I caution against such a shortcut. An Irish proverb might
apply here: The longest way round is the shortest way home.

What for?   As you may recall, this is the operative question used
to set up achievement-based objectives. Like the nonprofit groups in
New England and the Chilean health professionals, the Haitian
individuals were overworked and stressed. AIDS was not the only
disease they were struggling against. The political situation, as I have
said, was volatile. They did not intend to waste a moment in a
course that showed no immediacy. The achievement-based objectives from the generic course in Chapter Two were adapted therefore
for this critical context. By the end of the program, all participants
were expected to have

Reviewed current adult learning theory (Knowles and
Lewin) as it pertains to AIDS prevention education

Distinguished between monologue and dialogue

Practiced doing a learning needs assessment and identified
generative themes of a group for use in rural communities

Reviewed how groups work, with optimal participation for
use in clinic situations

Used and evaluated the principles and practices of popular
education in terms of how they can be used to design
AIDS education events

Practiced designing and using open questions

Practiced using and designing appropriate warm-ups (introductions to community health education events)

Reviewed the elements in a learning design

Practiced using the seven steps of planning in designing sessions

Practiced designing learning sessions in teams on AIDS using the principles and practices

Practiced making effective charts for these sessions

Practiced designing learning materials for AIDS education that engage learners through dialogue

Practiced teaching using their designs

Reviewed theory on feedback and practiced giving and getting feedback on designs and teaching

Designed two evaluation instruments, one for immediate and one for long-term evaluation of AIDS education courses

Used a wide variety of problem-posing teaching techniques, such as critical incidents, found objects, open questions, role plays, case studies, charts, synthesis, sociodrama, music, codes for analysis, snow cards, brainstorming, videos as codes, and closure

How? The Haitian course followed the generic program tasks while relating it to the AIDS agenda. All of the learning materials—including videos, handouts, and the program itself—were translated into French for the course and reviewed by a Haitian team for relevance and consistency. The cultural aspects of the translation were found to be very important. I worked with Dr. Maryse Narcisse of Save the Children, who was coordinator of the coalition. She had done the five-day training in popular education at Jubilee in Raleigh prior to preparing for the Haitian program. She was given the authority to make all decisions about the translation since she best knew the context and the culture.

The Design

As the first learning tasks—the introduction, warm-up, and review of program, objectives, content, and expectations—were worked through, it became evident that many of the coalition members were not clear about why they were present. In some cases, busy nurses had been told by their directors, "Go to this course!" without any explanation. Some of the doctors did not understand that this was not a course on the latest epidemiological AIDS research. They were confused.

The great advantage of the initial work on day one is that it makes such confusion explicit and provides the opportunity for dealing with it as well as possible. It is often tempting, under the duress of time and the exigency of working with busy professionals, to abandon this preparatory work and get right to the heart of the matter. The experience in Haiti showed how disastrous that would have been.

A traditional learning needs assessment using a telephone survey could not be done because there was no telephone connection at that time to the Central Plateau. There had been ample correspondence in preparation for the training course but, we discovered in this case, ample was not adequate. What might have been done instead? Narcisse and I might have taken a few days to visit some of the health clinics, talking to the doctors and nurses on site. We might have made a short video explaining our hopes for the course and sent it to each organization. Many of them read English, so we might have sent them each a copy of *Learning to Listen, Learning to Teach* (1994) and invited them to read it prior to the course.

I make this point to demonstrate that preparation is not only getting together materials that will work, but is also preparation of the learners. They will need to do the same thing with the health professionals they are teaching! Unfortunately, they were given a very poor model in Jubilee's failure to explore innovative learning needs assessment modes in this unique situation. Every situation is unique. The point is, in whatever way possible, to listen to the perspectives of a good sample of the adult learners ahead of time so that everyone is setting out on the same foot.

Roles and Tasks

Narcisse was the instructor in French for this course. My role was to sit by, quietly watching, offering what suggestions I could to Narcisse during breaks and at mealtime. The entire course was videotaped for the health professionals to take to their remote stations and use in training their community AIDS educators. On day two, the group began to coalesce and become excited about what they were learning. They suddenly saw how this new knowledge and these new skills and attitudes could inform their work in the villages and towns of the Central Plateau. The immediacy and relevance of the program were working.

Day one in such a course is always the most difficult as adult learners try to comprehend the whole picture and see their place in it. As the days progress, their energy rises and the job of the instructor actually gets easier. Sequence is an ally here, as the participants' involvement in each learning task gets more and more challenging and as they look to the formidable tasks of designing microteaching on day three and teaching on day four.

On day three, each of the design teams selected a topic related to the AIDS epidemic. All present were eager learners, needing to know what their colleagues had to offer. One team courageously dealt with the impact of new knowledge about AIDS on local culture, and the parallel impact of culture on the selection of ways of sharing new knowledge and skills. Another team used a video made in Haiti about a young woman who goes to Port au Prince to find work, gets infected with HIV, has a child who is also infected, and comes home to the Plateau to die. It is a powerful short film and the team used it as a code to inform their participative, problem-posing, popular education design. They did not show the entire film during their session, but only a clip that captured the poignancy of the situation. Their design set the adult learners in the room to the task of describing, analyzing, applying, and resolving the painful story by using the four open questions:

What do you see happening here?

Why do you think it happened?

If it happens in your community what problems will it cause?

What can we together do about it?

I was amazed to see how the feedback sessions after each teaching went right to the issue of transferring their new skills to the next level of health educators. These professionals realized they could not grasp all they needed to learn about the popular education approach in a five-day period and were demanding follow-up and support. The existing coalition would provide that support by conducting ongoing sessions of training and materials development. The participants agreed to bring their training designs for review at the monthly meetings of the coalition.

Narcisse discovered a new role for herself, coordinating the adult education efforts of the coalition. She would be the lead trainer and Jubilee would be one of the coalition's resource centers in the United States. During the political turmoil of 1994, the coalition had to endure lost boxes of books, downed telephone lines, scrambled faxes, and impassable roads. Events in 1995 brought new hope to Haiti. By then, eighteen of the members of the AIDS coalition were trained in popular education methods, and if it hadn't been for the coalition, these individual health professionals would have been very isolated indeed. Each subgroup in the coalition discovered anew in the training workshop how much they needed the others. Save the Children will send their nutrition specialist to a week-long train-the-trainer program in North Carolina, evidence of their esteem of the popular education approach.

Evaluation of the impact of this training course is longitudinal, that is, it is evident in what these health professionals are doing in their AIDS education training since the March 1994 session. The only indicators from the course itself are the participants' immediate planning of ways to meet the training needs of their health teams in the rural areas, their excitement about the perceived potential of the popular education approach, and their planned use of the coalition meetings to review designs and training events. Notice that each of the groups described so far independently set up such a coalition for continued study of popular education.

YOUR TURN

What do you see as the role of a research and training center? How can demands be made on such centers from the field so that their efforts (materials, designs, research) are fully accessible? Please call Jubilee (919/847–3804; Fax 919/870–0599) or write the publisher or Jubilee (1221 Moultrie Court, Raleigh, NC 27615) with responses to these questions and any other ideas you might have.

Education for Critical Thinking is the engaging title of one of Paulo Freire's classic texts. In Haiti, education for critical thinking around the issue of preventing AIDS is the only kind that works, offering a theory of transformation and inviting participants to use this transforming process themselves. The Coalition for the Prevention of AIDS and STDs in Haiti will be making qualitative and quantitative reports on the spread of AIDS and other sexually transmitted diseases in Haiti. If education is a real tool in their medical kits to transform the thinking and behavior of adults and if the popular education approach works for them, the epidemiological results will be evident. Haiti is one crucible in which the potential of this approach for teaching about AIDS among rural adults is being tested by fire.

6

Transforming the Culture of Teaching

Training in Literacy Programs

People as beings 'in a situation' find themselves rooted in temporal-spatial conditions which mark them and which they also mark. They will tend to reflect on their own 'situationality' to the extent that they are challenged by it to act on it. Human beings are because they are in a situation. And they will be more the more they not only critically reflect upon their existence, but critically act upon it.

—Paulo Freire (1993, p. 90)

Nothing is more oppressive for an adult in the United States than being unable to read. Literacy is the basis of personal power. Literacy Volunteers of America (LVA) and Laubach Literacy Action (LLA) recognize that fact and invite men and women, in a very personal dialogue with a tutor, to not only reflect on the problem but critically act on it by learning how to read their own stories. LVA and LLA are the two major literacy resources in the United States. Both have training programs for volunteer tutors, materials for tutor training, and materials for the actual literacy training, and each maintains a press that provides back-up and support literature for their constituents. Both LVA and LLA provide local organizations, usually volunteer groups, with the support they need in both management and educational processes. Both have headquarters in Syracuse, New York, and share a history of as well as a desire for excellence and careful extension to meet the needs of those who must learn to read and write in order to survive in the United States.

LLA and LVA were each planning an effort to redesign their organizational train-the-trainers courses and their tutor training materials. They invited Jubilee to do a week-long course with the top training planners of both organizations in January 1993. Asking the "why" question during the planning phase resulted in the following situation analysis:

> Both literacy organizations are doing excellent work. We know, however, that the present train-the-trainers program and the training materials for both trainers and tutors do not adequately reflect current research in adult learning. While they will continue to be two different organizations, with distinct organizational approaches, they hope to maintain a common ground of principles and practices that is based on the latest research about how adults learn.

Preparation

Jubilee agreed to this contract two months prior to the week set for the training course, which provided just about enough time to prepare. When each organization sent Jubilee the list of senior staff whom they had invited to attend, all of them were surveyed during lengthy phone calls. All participants were contacted, not just a sample. All of these individuals were decision makers in their organizations, and it was important to know their perspective on this strategic change in direction.

LLA and LVA's contract with Jubilee did indeed represent a change in direction. I had been familiar with these organizations' approaches to literacy training for years. While it was a great honor to be invited, it was a challenge to present Jubilee's conceptualization of current research as an open system for the leaders of these organizations to use and adapt as they could into their organizational culture.

All of the people surveyed were delighted at the opportunity to talk. The survey questions were simple and direct:

Tell us something about your history in this organization.

What is your present role?

Tell us about something you are proud of having done in this organization.

Why do you see this training course for senior staff as necessary at this time?

What one achievement do you want to come out of this for you? For your organization?

Two busy executives who could not talk by phone sent typed, comprehensive responses to all the questions. All of the participants were intensely earnest about the project, although everyone mentioned that they hated to give up the amount of time for which the course was being designed. The course would last for five days. There would be twenty participants—ten from each literacy organization. Both organizations sent to Jubilee all their literature, including large training manuals and curricula for their tutor training and training-the-trainers programs. They also sent copies of the videos they used in training.

YOUR TURN

What else might have been done to discover the culture of each organization and their learning needs and competencies? How about attending one of their train-the-trainers courses? How about going to the local literacy group and watching a tutor at work with an individual student? How about talking to an individual student who was being tutored by either an LVA or LLA tutor, and talking to tutors about their perception of their training? How about a survey of a sample of LVA and LLA trainers around the country? What else would you suggest might have been done so as not to leave any stones unturned in this preparation? One cannot do too much.

With "who," "where," "when," and "why" already determined, an examination of the generic program presented in Chapter Two revealed that major decisions needed to be made about the rest of the seven steps—"what," "what for," and "how." How should the two diverse organizational cultures be dealt with? If microteaching teams were to be set up, should they be organizational or heterogeneous? What content was vital and what might be omitted to deal with the organizations' immediate need to transform their training programs? Having the generic model is always a great help. It was clear, however, that a great deal had to be done to it to adapt it to this unique situation.

A draft program based on the seven steps of planning, the survey results, and the generic model was designed and sent to the course organizers from LVA and LLA. They reviewed the draft and made suggestions that were incorporated. The next step was to prepare the learning materials:

A program book containing all the learning tasks and relevant materials

A library of resources

Charts containing all the learning tasks, objectives, content, and daily programs

Name cards for the five tables of four we intended to use (at the beginning of the session, each table group contained participants from both LVA and LLA)

Jubilee certificates for all participants

The Design

In spite of the telephone survey and Jubilee's constant contact with the course organizers, participants were visibly reluctant to be at such a course for a whole week. They knew how to do training. They were long experienced in doing for their literacy volunteers just what Jubilee was doing: designing and leading a train-the-trainers course. They all had tons of work on their desks and deadlines winking at them from their computer calendars. We soon realized we would have to be very convincing on day one if we were going to get them to come back to even day two!

The course opened with warm welcomes and speeches by the presidents of both organizations. They corroborated the importance of this collaborative effort to the overall development of the literacy movement in the United States. Just how tentative the participants were emerged during the initial tasks—the warm-up, the program review, and the expectations. While they might already be critically *reflecting* upon their situation, they were apprehensive about the effort involved in critically *acting* on it.

Any program is cumulative. This course is especially so. By day five, it is always recognized by participants as excellent and useful, but on day one they have to make an act of faith. I stress that fact here to encourage those who will adapt this model and perhaps feel some of this inevitable fear on the first day. Jubilee's faith in the model is operative, but it does not obviate the trepidation of facing a group of twenty senior literacy specialists and administrators from the two major literacy organizations in the United States. I am always nervous at the opening of any training course, and I usually have to give myself time to walk around the block a few times before the session starts. I walked a mile in the snow in Syracuse that first morning!

Once the energy in the small groups was stimulated by their response to the first learning tasks, the instructors' apprehension diminished. One of the participants asked my colleague Joan and me to join her for lunch on day two. She shared her concern about some of our awkward moments and evident lack of control. As she put it, "I have done what you are doing many times. I do not see that you are demonstrating greater skill than I already have." While this was tough personal feedback, it was an important learning moment. We were not there to demonstrate our skills, but to share with them a new model that could be useful both to trainers and tutors, who would come to it with diverse skill levels. We thanked her for the feedback, acknowledging our own inadequacies, which we might or might not be able to amend. We spoke about the operator factor in the whole process and urged her to stay on board to get the whole picture of the new process and all the content. She did so, and thanked us on the last day for both listening to her concerns and inviting her to continue.

Virtually all of the learning tasks in the generic model were used in this course. Each task was designed to invite participants' consideration of how it would apply in their training of literacy volunteers. They spent a great deal of time reflecting on how they presently did whatever was being taught: communication skills, learning needs assessment, evaluation, or design. The learning tasks invited this comparison without any defense of either form.

On day three when they formed small groups to do microteaching, the participants agreed to work in their respective organizations rather than to form mixed teams. This decision made sense, since there is a recognizable educational culture in each organization that needed to be respected. This was an example of how important it is never to decide for adults what they can decide for themselves.

The microteaching in this session was memorable, offering examples of problem-posing training incidents that came directly from the participants' own experience. One problem-posing role play that demonstrated a tutor who used none of the principles and practices of popular education raised such antagonism from the participants who were playing the part of the learners, the instructors were afraid their response would be violent. The tutor just barely escaped tar and feathers. Here was a demonstration of their success in using the affective in their training design!

Roles and Tasks

Since many of the participants in this training course were experienced in one form of what was being taught, the role of the instructors became even more explicitly that of resource persons. On the basis of the feedback offered, we knew we were not demonstrating what they considered top-quality facilitating. Our errors were a blessing in disguise, since we did not want them to do their literacy training exactly as we had done in this course. They would need to adapt the course to their own organizational cultures if it was to be useful as their new approach to literacy training. At each table, individuals with more experience than others in the design of train-the-trainers programs and materials were resource people to their peers. Although many of the concepts of the principles and practices of popular education were old and familiar, the language was new to everyone, so they often chose to translate the concepts into their own cultural literacy jargon.

Part of the role of the instructors was to keep the energy up and the course moving along into the microteaching and through the first feedback sessions. These feedback sessions were sensitive, not only because the participants were working in front of peers but also because of the diversity of the two organizations present. The job of the instructors was to lavish affirmation on all efforts and still to challenge them to move beyond what they already knew so well. It was not an enviable role! A training course like this is no tea party.

Immediacy was the watchword as the groups gathered to consider next steps on the final day of the course. Two new curricula were being developed, one LLA, one LVA, and deadlines were approaching. A train-the-trainers course for the new management curriculum recently produced by LVA was coming up in a month. The designer and author of this curriculum was an enthusiastic participant in the training course. She was determined to redo the management training curriculum using the principles and practices of popular education. The annual LVA national convention was imminent and local trainings were ongoing. A new tutor training manual was being considered by LVA. All of these events and materials would be affected by the training course. At the time of this writing, LVA has thoroughly revamped their materials and processes to incorporate popular education principles and practices throughout. It was a pleasant surprise to hear reports from various levels within the organizations of the changes effected in programs and processes. Language changed. They spoke of achievement-based objectives and the seven steps of planning, of immediacy and relevance, of the need to engage the learners. Again, evaluation is longitudinal. Ongoing and cumulative changes can be documented and experienced in each new training course.

Both organizations are growing in their use of the popular education approach and in their adaptation and development of the principles behind it. It is important to record that neither literacy organization took one step toward use of this problem-posing, participative, accountable model that was not critiqued—not because it was so very different from what they had been doing for decades, but because they knew what a significant change it would effect in their programs. As Freire's epigraph to this chapter indicates, LVA and LLA saw they could *be* more as literacy organizations by not only critically reflecting on their existence but by critically acting on their problems to enhance their services to literacy students around the country.

7

Rebuilding Faith in Teaching

Training in a Substance Abuse Program

Dialogue further requires an intense faith in humankind, faith in their power to make and remake, to create and re-create, faith in their vocation to be more fully human (which is not the privilege of an elite but the birthright of all). Faith in people is an a priori requirement for dialogue; "the dialogical man" believes in others even before he meets them face to face.
—Paulo Freire, 1993, p. 71

This chapter contains an abundance of lessons learned in the example of a training course for professionals working with substance abusers at a veterans' affairs (VA) hospital. Many of the hospital's veteran clients returned again and again for treatment that is lengthy, expensive, and demanding of the staff. These health professionals needed to strengthen their faith in this suffering segment of humankind, to fortify their own humility as well as hone their skills, and to relearn the uses of inclusion as they worked as a team. Their roles in relation to one another and in relation to their patients needed clarifying as they recognized themselves as wounded healers.

Preparation

Rodrigo Escalona was introduced in Chapter Three as a psychiatrist who had studied at Duke University's Medical School and gained his first exposure to popular education as leader of a training course held at the Universidad Católica Medical School in Santiago, Chile. He was deeply impressed by the short training experience. From there he came to the drug and alcohol unit of a Veterans' Affairs hospital. After some time as staff psychiatrist, he suggested to the director, Colin Quinn, that the entire staff of the unit might do such a training. The staff included educators as well as psychiatric social workers, psychiatrists, nurses, and aides. Their central job is to provide a healing education, inviting veterans who have been crippled by drugs and alcohol to learn how to walk again. In all their preparation as medical professionals, few of them had ever had put to them such questions as, How do adults learn? and What does it mean to know something? Escalona and Quinn agreed that it was time to develop this area of their staff's diverse skills, and they invited Jubilee to design and facilitate the program.

Twenty-five people worked on the unit. A group of twelve were selected to participate in the training course, leaving the others "on the floor" to maintain the program for the duration of the training program. Jubilee staff read all they could about the program, and all twelve participants completed a learning needs assessment survey that included the following questions: What is your role in the unit? What is the hardest part of the job for you? How do you spell "success" in your job? Having read over the draft plan for the week-long training, what do you personally hope to achieve during the week?

I spent two days on the unit prior to the training week, meeting all the staff and interviewing each of the twelve participants. Three tasks are vital to learning needs assessment: to ask, to study, and to observe. My site visit moved this particular learning needs assessment from ask and study to observe, and gave both Jubilee and the unit staff a better sense of what could happen during the week of training.

Escalona had prepared a case study from the file of a single anonymous patient who had come back to the unit four times over the previous two years. The case study provided a sense of the difficult educational and healing task the unit's team had to do. A room large enough for three tables with four participants at each was selected at a nearby hotel for the training site. It was away from the medical center, yet near enough for emergency calls. A week-long course demands the perfect site: a large, airy, cool room, distant from the workplace.

The Design

The generic training program was used with few changes. On the first day, there was the familiar resistance to the prospect of a week away from their workplace. As one nurse put it, "The work will pile up and not be done by anyone else." I know of no way to avoid this resistance. Also, it is not the job of the instructors to resist the resistance, as illustrated in the story of the resistant Chilean physician in Chapter Three. The facilitator's job in the first few learning tasks is to quickly let the adult learners see that what is being offered is substantive and will be immediately useful to them.

The participants' expectations, elicited in Task 2, manifested their relationship with the veterans who came to them for healing and education. Most of the participants had worked on the unit for many years and had experienced the repeated return of many of their patients. Such a phenomenon could give anyone reason to doubt that adults can learn. It soon became apparent that this training course would need to include some basic training in hopefulness and the "faith in humankind" that Freire speaks about.

As they moved through the learning tasks, working in small self-selected groups, the participants were also dealing explicitly with their own history together. Much of what they were learning about communication, needs assessment, respect, and listening was relevant to their mutual learning as co-workers, colleagues, and friends. As a medical unit, they were the "dream team": well-educated, experienced, and skillful. They recognized throughout the week that they themselves needed the healing and education they offered their patients. Everyone listened with awe as they told their stories and recognized themselves as *wounded healers*.

Carl Jung (1969) once remarked that the patients he got were the ones he needed for his own spiritual work. This VA hospital team discovered that the skills they were learning and practicing in the course could be used among themselves as well as with their patients. The composition of the small groups changed each day through their own self-selection. In the educational process I had observed during my preliminary site visit, there was no small group work. All group work was in a single large group with a facilitator who clearly was the locus of control. As the course participants worked fruitfully in the small groups during the training course, they began to consider the possibility of using small groups in working with their patients.

Both the Kate Farrell story (Task 8) and the examples of monologue offered in Task 9 for their analysis were troublesome to all of these individuals, who were used to using a monologue approach in their work with clients. *We teach the way we were taught!* They argued that it was their responsibility to "cover" immense amounts of material with their patients and they therefore had to use monologue. The fact that patients returned to the unit was a quiet testimony to the futility of some of their current educational practices. During the week, they were urged to examine alternatives, to try them in the safe environment provided by this course, and then to decide later, back on the unit, what they might include in their work.

In order to make hope a more cogent factor in their future work, a special learning task was added to the generic model that invited participants to consider explicitly how they might use the principles and practices of popular education in their work as a team and in their efforts with the veterans. In the review task entitled "Put your cards on the table!" these health professionals were invited to reflect on ways they could use each of the principles and practices they selected in their work with the veterans and how such use would be a new procedure in the unit. This task enabled them to raise some tough questions about the established programs and practices of the unit.

Roles and Relationships in the Team

The director of the unit took full part in the training course. This was a vital factor in the success and fruitfulness of the program. Since he was there as a full member of the team and as a very active participant in the small group work, the others knew he supported this new approach to their work. The only people who cannot learn through this approach are those who are sure they already know, who do not harbor an honest question in their hearts. Quinn manifested how much he honors those honest questions, and in doing so he not only learned himself but enabled others on his dream team to learn with him. As subjects of their own learning, both director and staff clarified through this process the roles and relationships they wanted to have in their work.

The job of the instructors was to set the learning tasks, sit still, be quiet, and listen. We coordinated the participants' sharing at the end of each task, but they were no doubt teaching one another the content of the training program. All of the staff members—physicians, nurses, social workers, and aides—began to feel their potential for both listening and teaching. The tone in the room changed palpably from day one to day three; it became both more serious and more playful, and more attentive. The learning tasks they had accomplished proved to them that this learning was meaningful. The resistance of day one disappeared like morning mist in the bright sun.

To do the difficult task of design and microteaching, these men and women who had a long history together, who had often failed to appreciate one another, formed design teams that showed their new relationships: a social worker with a physician, a nurse with an aide. It was as if they were testing the limits of their dream team. Each team selected content for their microteaching that they wanted to teach their peers. Their learning needs assessment proved to them how much the group needed to learn about AIDS prevention, about the dynamics of small-group work, and about the history of Alcoholics Anonymous, which is the program of choice in this unit. True to the keen intelligence of this group, they used a wide selection of techniques in their designs, and the feedback session was rich with considerations of how this approach could be used in their group sessions with the veterans.

Leadership emerged in the group, as expected, but from a surprising source. The popular education approach has proved to evoke leadership and full expression from articulate participants who are not always heard in their work group. Being included by design rouses energy in those who may have felt excluded in the past. The participation and contributions of nurses and aides in this course was refreshing to all. A sociodrama on AIDS led by two team members brought us all to tears. Because the learning tasks throughout the course called on ideas, feelings, and action, the members of this diverse team were able to relate to one another at a new level.

Escalona was not a participant in this first session since he was responsible for maintaining the program at the VA hospital. He was, however, hearing exciting reviews of the course from the participants each evening. He received kudos from his teammates for setting up the program. Their hopefulness for new levels of communication was growing.

The director of the hospital's department of psychiatry not only approved of the course, he also encouraged Quinn to carry it out. He asked, "How can such events become a part of the rhythm of a busy hospital?" Medical professionals keep up with the journals in their discipline and spend time at conferences hearing learned papers read on the epidemiology and pathologies with which they work. How can the pathologies in working groups, the epidemiology of dissatisfaction and neglect that often infects professional teams, be regularly addressed? As noted in Chapter Two in regard to team-leading the training course, the powerful demand, "Attention must be paid!" from Arthur Miller's *Death of a Salesman* (1949), holds for all working situations. Again, the principle of inclusion should be the guide. If professionals do not pay attention to one another within the service group, how can they adequately pay attention to their clients or patients?

In his revealing book *A Whole New Life* (1994), Reynolds Price questions the manifest lack of human courtesy he experienced from high-level medical staff during his bout with cancer. He celebrated the gentle courtesy he felt from porters, nurses aides, and waiters in the hospital commissary. This training course enabled health professionals to examine the community they created and the quality of communication and mutual support among all members of the team.

The demands made on staff in the drug and alcohol unit of the VA hospital do not allow for much structured reflection on their process. This one week had been an opportunity for some of the professional staff, with a wide mix of roles represented, to take time to reflect upon their actions as educators and healers. All of them acknowledged the need for such reflection, even if they showed resistance at first to the "loss" of a week of work. A week-long program cannot perform miracles. There is the need for a second course, to review new approaches that are being tried and to share problems with the implementation of the principles and practices in the workplace. Budgets rarely allow for a second course, because of the prevailing misconception, "Tell them once and they know." Such a misconception works at two levels in this case. When it prevails in the treatment of veterans crippled by drugs and alcohol, it results in recidivism; when it prevails in the staff development efforts of the unit, it can result in inadequate support for new learning.

When this team meets to review their processes, they might use the four assumption questions cited in Chapter One:

1. Who am I?
2. What is the world?
3. How can we live and work together?
4. What is "to know"?

As they review the popular education responses to these questions, they can be reminded of their week-long experience of inclusion, of clarified roles and relationships, and of their sharing of personal stories that manifested their sense of feeling humbled by their job, of being wounded healers.

YOUR TURN

You are director of this unit. A tidal wave of veterans pours into the unit daily. Always at maximum patient capacity, the unit is often at the breaking point. Nurses often do not take vacation due them because of the workload. The constant return of patients is demoralizing to staff who see this as a failure of the program. How do you nourish your professional staff in a regular and satisfactory way? What can you do based on this training program to establish an ongoing process of staff development?

Jubilee has heard from the new director of the unit that she wants to do the same training course with the other half of the staff, including herself. One of the physicians described the effect of the course in this way: their classes with clients are now "softer." When everyone on staff has done the training course, quantitative evidence can be sought in decreasing numbers of clients coming back to the unit. If the replication of this training process throughout the VA system is desirable, both quantitative and qualitative evidence must be shown to decision makers.

8

Making Time for Training

A Community Development Bank Invests in Learning

> To exist humanly is to name the world, to change it. Once named, the world in its turn reappears to the namers as a problem, and requires of them a new naming. . . . Dialogue is the encounter between men, mediated by the world, in order to name the world.
>
> —Paulo Freire (1993, p.69)

In rural Arkansas depressed towns abound. Main Street is often a maze of boarded up shops, with worn "for sale" signs rusting in the windows. Southern Development Bancorporation, a community development bank established to give credit and build wealth in distressed rural communities, included a microenterprise program in their affiliate in Pine Bluff called the Good Faith Fund (GFF).

GFF of Pine Bluff has as its purpose to increase incomes, assets, and entrepreneurial opportunities for local residents. Close to 85 percent of the active members of Good Faith Fund are minority, 65 percent are female, and 20 percent are still receiving public assistance. GFF has a Welfare Transition Program to make self-employment a legitimate and viable option for welfare recipients and to offer the loans, training, and support group assistance needed to enable them to become self-sufficient through self-employment.

GFF, as a microenterprise program, is essentially an alternative financial institution and community education organization: small peer-lending groups, staff meetings, community orientation sessions to recruit new members, GFF members' meetings, the publication *Sidelines*, a newsletter for members—all serve to educate the people in the ten rural counties in southeastern Arkansas where GFF staff work. All staff are group facilitators, trainers, and teachers, as well as case managers, loan representatives, and administrators.

There is a Business Orientation and Training (BOT) curriculum offered to all GFF prospective peer-lending members. In seven three-hour sessions the loan representatives/trainers from GFF teach marketing strategies, organizational issues, budgeting and financial management, and borrowing and lending protocols, and examine possible new enterprise ideas. A second program, NOVA, is a twelve-week program for those still on Aid to Families with Dependent Children (AFDC) who wish to begin their own enterprise. This is a program for members on AFDC and other forms of public assistance that aims to get them off that public assistance and onto their own established income.

As you can see from this brief description, popular education is what these men and women do in their community development bank microenterprise program. The director of the Good Faith Fund, Julia Vindasius, invited Jubilee to do a training session with the staff. She and I together planned a program that would work with all staff from the ten rural counties. Time was a major issue, as staff had obligations to borrowers groups and ongoing programs. We agreed that I would be available in Pine Bluff for a week, doing a one-day training session. A new staff person who would be directing the NOVA program would come to North Carolina to study at the week-long training program run by Jubilee.

Preparation

The learning needs assessment for this train-the-trainers program began with my reading all the information sent to me about the Good Faith Fund and its complex operations. I sent a survey form to each of the GFF staff with these questions:

What is your perception of your job at GFF?

What do you see as your strengths as a trainer?

What are the areas of training you wish to improve?

Everyone sent full responses which described their situations, and I was sent videotapes of each staff person doing one session of one of the GFF trainings or group meetings. These clearly showed me how the staff were teaching. The materials they used, micro-enterprise development videos, textbooks, and training manuals, are all designed from a more formal educational perspective.

GFF invited Jubilee because they wanted to teach from a more popular education approach. Their assumptions were the same as those shared in Chapter One. They wanted to be catalysts for the personal and professional development of these rural men and women. The training approach they were using as seen in their videos and in my examination of the materials they used could be enhanced by a few simple principles and practices from popular education. They really were searching for an approach that stimulated creativity, used small groups well, invited critical thinking, offered occasion for frequent application of what was being learned, and was based on dialogue among peers.

The staff surveys all mentioned problems with "motivation" of adult students who come to class tired in the evening after lots of work at home. The staff spoke as teachers to describe their needs: "I need to *call on* shy people; I want to be more faithful to the *training manual*, I need to be careful about zooming through *the agenda*. . . ." They indicated that they knew exactly what they needed to learn in this popular education training. They all stressed their desire to learn how to listen more effectively.

As Julia and I began together to design a set of achievement-based objectives which would move their training practice toward their own felt needs and aspirations, we kept stumbling over the issue of time. Like the other not-for-profit groups described in Chapter Four, these were busy staff members. They were so busy training, they could not find time for learning how to use popular education approaches in their training. This is a perennial problem. I am a good example of this syndrome. Rather than take time from my "busy schedule" (writing this book!) to go to a training program to learn the exciting services my computer program offers, I use one hundredth of the capability of the software. Who said it: time you old beggar man!

Congruence is a guide to the problem we faced. These staff members worked hard to cover the material they had to teach to new microenterprise venturers and new borrowers' groups in the time they were allotted. It was my duty to avoid trying to "cover" too much in the time we had together. My modeling would try to demonstrate that less is more.

We worked out a program that enabled me to work with each staff member individually, and to have the new staff member attend the five-day program in North Carolina. Copies of *Learning to Listen, Learning to Teach* (1994) were made available to all staff members.

As we considered the content (the "what") and the objectives (the "what for") of this short train-the-trainers program, we had to work only with the essentials because of the time frame. I decided to model the approach by working with them on only four achievement-based objectives, hoping these would so inform their teaching that they would invite us back for more! By the end of our time we would have:

Reviewed current adult learning theory using Knowles and Lewin

Distinguished between monologue (banking) and dialogue (problem-posing) as approaches to learning (the Freire concept), using the Seven Steps of Planning

Practiced designing and using open questions

Examined the BOT curriculum with reference to some of the principles and practices of popular education

The content we agreed on then, was: adult learning theory; open questions; monologue (banking) and dialogue (problemposing), principles and practices of popular education.

YOUR TURN

If you went back to the generic training course in Chapter Two, what would you choose to include in a short train-thetrainers course like this, when the trainers being trained clearly need to learn and practice much more than time permits? Should I have concentrated on how a group works instead of making direct application to any one program such as BOT? What else would you see as essential to include? Why? How much of a compromise about time is too great a compromise?

As I modeled leading learning tasks in a short train-the-trainers program, we put up cards containing some of the principles and practices as they were demonstrated. During the dialogue I had with each of the trainers around the video of a training session each had done, I worked to affirm what they were doing well, and to build one new idea or skill, for example: "How about making that question an open question?" or "How could you affirm that response from that woman?" Even if the training manual they were using asks a closed question that looks for a "right" answer, the GFF trainer can adapt the manual to the popular education practice of open questions, inviting critical thinking and personal application. "How about asking the group for parallel situations in Arkansas to those they are seeing on the textbook video?" This would show respect for the situations of these particular people, honor their themes, and acknowledge their perspectives. "How about naming *one* skill learners can practice, rather than many?" This would lead to affirmation of their success with a single skill, and build confidence.

It was my task to set up action goals these staff could accomplish. They proved, in their responses to an evaluation survey six months after the event that asked: What use have you made in your training and group work with GFF of the staff development event in September 1994 when Jubilee came to work with us? that they were using those principles and practices they learned in ways that assured engagement, accountability, and respect for their adult learners. The new staff person, who attended the five-day session, was excited and motivated to use this approach in the NOVA program.

Lessons Learned

While it is a hard stance for Jubilee to take, we have decided not to do train-the-trainers programs if we do not have five days for staff to learn and *practice* new skills, new knowledge, and new attitudes. The constant struggle to deal with the foreshortened time frames of busy GFF staff diminished their learning potential and frustrated everyone. We do not do a good service to groups by offering to teach more than we can in a short time. I urge readers to be firm, more firm than I have been in the past, in determining how much time a group will give you. If the time they can offer is too short, I negotiate to work at a later date when there is more time available.

A favorite axiom of ours is: "Do you wish to have a baby? Do you have nine months?" Any time less than nine months can mean years and years of pain and trouble. The same truth holds for training trainers.

A second lesson learned about training trainers was the importance of the preparation and needs assessment. Because of the videotapes and the surveys, and my reading about GFF, I felt competent to decide with the staff what should be selected for the one-day training program. I realize anew that one never does too much preparation.

Finally, I realized again how appropriate this approach is to community education efforts. The learners at GFF needed to review their knowledge and skills about how to work effectively together in small groups, how to have rich and fruitful dialogue, how to respect and listen to one another, how to develop confidence in their own perspectives, how to learn technical skills and knowledge in relation to their own businesses or trades or lives, and how to discover and use resources within their grasp. These are skills modeled as well as taught in this popular education approach.

While that staff development effort included their reading *Learning to Listen, Learning to Teach*, how much of a change in their behavior was effected by their reading that book? How much of a change in *your* behavior will be effected by your reading this book? The prevailing lesson learned in this experience is the need for time for dialogue, for working together to develop needed skills, knowledge, and attitudes.

GFF wisely sent three staff members the next year to the five-day course in North Carolina. Their opportunity to enhance their skills even more in that course was directly related to the time factor. Throughout the next year, the GFF staff continued to look for opportunities to use and develop what they had learned in each aspect of their work together and with the organization's members.

YOUR TURN

Here is a critical incident for you to mull over: An industry with a large factory wants to train their training staff in the principles and practices of popular education, in order to develop more critical thinking and independence in the line staff at the factory. The CEO and the director of training of the industry invite you to give their twelve trainers a one-day course in popular education theory and practice. They pay well, at an industrial rate. What is your response to them? Why?

As more and more legislation that promotes interdependence and a balanced budget stresses re-training and training for new efforts, the work of groups like the Good Faith Fund becomes central to the educational efforts of a state or nation. These principles and practices of popular education can be useful in developing even more accountable, engaging, successful community education programs. It's time to give time to the work of training trainers in this approach.

9

The Challenge of Design

Developing a Program for Community Volunteers

The dialogical theory of action does not involve a Subject, who dominates by virtue of conquest, and a dominated object. Instead there are Subjects who meet to name the world in order to transform it.

—Paulo Freire (1993, p. 148)

This chapter portrays a challenging situation calling for the training of trainers. It will give you the opportunity to apply all that you have reviewed in this book so far as you examine this design for an appropriate, effective, accountable train-the-trainers course for a group of police trainers. While this is a hypothetical situation, it is not an unlikely one.

The Seven Steps

The design process begins with the seven steps of popular education.

Who? Twelve police officers who have a heavy training schedule mainly but not only in the urban communities of this large city are selected to participate in the course. All twelve are sent copies of *Learning to Listen, Learning to Teach* and a needs assessment survey consisting of three questions:

1. What are you proud of in your training programs for the community?

2. What are some of the problems you face in training community volunteers?

3. After reading *Learning to Listen, Learning to Teach*, what would you like to learn in this train-the-trainers course for community educators?

The officers' responses to the needs assessment survey indicate that they do not share the chief's analysis of the problem of attrition among their volunteer trainees. They all believe that people drop out because the job that volunteers are expected to do is too difficult and too dangerous. Their expectations of this training course are low.

Each officer is interviewed for five minutes by telephone; also interviewed are the chief, his assistant, and six citizen volunteers who have completed a safety officer training course. Jubilee attends a series of trainings for citizen volunteer safety officers and there observes both the content and the process. Since the police officers always train in uniform, it is deemed appropriate for Jubilee staff to dress conservatively for the training course. All of the issues raised when preparing such a course are related to respect. The results of the needs assessment are included in the training materials for the course given to the participants.

Why? The police chief of a large North Carolina city has a cadre of twelve training officers, all experienced law enforcement personnel, who work with community volunteers. Since these police officers have all been trained in a paramilitary fashion, they naturally use the same approach in training community safety volunteers. That approach, they find, does not work. Volunteers begin a course of training, and then drop out at the rate of close to 50 percent. After reading *Learning to Listen, Learning to Teach* (1994), the chief decides that the training officers need to learn a new approach to providing community education—the popular education approach to adult education. He calls Jubilee for a proposal for a training course for these police officers.

When? The course is planned to last for five days, for a total of forty hours. The chief is loath to give these five days, and the officers also are concerned about their pressing duties. This is not a negotiable issue. These individuals need to examine their working assumptions and to identify and try on new ones; they need to not only learn about skills, knowledge, and attitudes congruent with a new approach, but also to practice these. This takes time.

Where? It is determined that the course will not take place in the police training center where the officers hold all their usual training sessions. Instead, it will take place in a community center that has a comfortable room with tables for four, a TV and VCR, two flip charts, and a video camera. The officers often do their community volunteer training in such centers. While it would be useful for these men and women to see how their training site could be used in the popular education approach, the purpose of this course is not to transform all their training programs, but to focus on the one program for community safety volunteers. A course site in the community therefore makes sense.

What? The police officers need to learn the following skills, knowledge, and attitudes:

Skills

How to motivate citizen volunteers

How to describe and analyze the current volunteer training program

How to communicate adult to adult

How to use a video effectively

How to use a flip chart

How to design training sessions

How to give and get feedback

How to set achievement-based objectives

How to design and use open questions

Knowledge

How adults learn (Knowles's research)

The difference between monologue and dialogue

Task and group maintenance needs of a group

Guidelines for feedback

Berne's communication theory

The difference between a consultative and deliberative
voice

Attitudes

Respect

Confidence

Humor

Note that the content selected immediately addresses the officers' felt needs. These police officers are being sent by the chief to this training. They are not coming voluntarily. It is imperative to prove to them early on that what they will be learning will be useful in their work.

What for? By the end of the five days, all the police training officers will have:

Skills

Identified ways to motivate citizen volunteers

Practiced describing and analyzing a training program to
enhance it

Practiced adult to adult communication

Named ways and practiced how to use a video effectively

Practiced using flip charts effectively

Designed training sessions using the popular education
approach

Practiced giving and getting feedback using the guidelines

Set achievement-based objectives for their designs

Designed and used open questions

Distinguished a consultative and a deliberative voice

Knowledge

Examined how adults learn (Knowles's research)

Identified the difference between monologue and dialogue

Named task and group maintenance needs of a group

Reviewed guidelines for feedback

Reviewed Berne's communication theory

Attitudes

Practiced respect

Developed confidence

Used humor throughout

These achievement-based objectives are what the police officers will do with the content they will be learning. This design has fewer objectives than the generic design in Chapter Two. It has been customized for these particular participants.

How? Step 7, How, includes the learning tasks and materials. These will be described in detail in the pages that follow, with notes about why the particular tasks are being done with this group of adult learners.

When the participants arrive at the course site, they find name cards on tables for groups of three. The tables are arranged arbitrarily for the first learning tasks. Each participant receives a notebook containing the complete design of the program, including all the learning tasks, the cards listing the seven steps of planning, and a set of cards listing the fifty principles and practices of popular education. The flip charts needed for the learning tasks of day one are on the easels, and the video is set to begin playing exactly where it is needed. Good food and drink are available throughout the day. All of these incidental preparations are part of the model, showing respect and assuring inclusion.

Day one begins with a welcome (which I usually script in order to make sure I include everything I need to say). The purpose of the welcome is to invite participants' trust in the presenters as teachers and in the program. They will trust the process by the end of the week.

Task 1: Welcome, Program and Objectives Review, Expectations

The Welcome   Welcome! I want to thank the chief for his invitation to work with all of you on ways to strengthen the training of community safety officer volunteers. Thank you all for your cooperation in the learning needs assessment, in returning the surveys, and in doing the telephone interviews. The information obtained in those processes is on page fifteen of your course notebook. Thanks also for permitting us to visit your training sessions.

We will be working rather informally at these four tables of three, and you will change the table groups often to get the opportunity to work with all of your colleagues. We will take lots of breaks, but please get coffee or food as you need it, and take your own breaks as needed.

Our task is to model with you this week a new approach to community education. You can decide at the end what you can use of it in your community education efforts with the volunteer safety officers. As questions arise about either the usefulness of this approach or the congruence of what we do here to what we are teaching, please ask them immediately.

You will receive a complete report of these sessions, so your note taking is up to you. I want you to know that we have done this program in more than forty countries around the world, with a wide variety of trainers. You are in good company! Let's begin.

Review of Program Objectives and Content   At your tables, read the content and objectives of the program, marking the material as you read. Look ahead at the learning tasks. What are your questions? Name these questions at your table, and we'll respond as we can.

Day One

Welcome, Program and Objectives Review, Expectations

Analysis of Community Safety Officer Program

How Adults Learn

How to Motivate Citizens

Monologue and Dialogue

Generative Themes of a Community and Needs Assessment

Cognitive, Affective, and Psychomotor Aspects of Learning

How Groups Work

Evaluation and Closure

Day Two

Welcome and Warm-Up

Review of Readings in Learning to Listen, Learning to Teach

Communications Theory

Using a Video in Problem-Posing Adult Learning

Open Questions

Demonstration of a Popular Education Design

Designing Together

Evaluation and Closure

Day Three

Welcome and Warm-Up

Design in Teams of Two

Microteaching and Feedback

Day Four

Back to the Drawing Board

Second Microteaching and Feedback

Day Five

Synthesis

Redesigning the Curriculum

Evaluation and Closure

Expectations At your table, name your personal expectations of this week. Write each one on a card and put it on this chart of expectations. We'll hear them all.

At this point, the instructors explain that participants' expectations inform but do not form the program. They also make the distinction between a consultative and deliberative voice in a group, noting that suggestions (consultative voice) are welcome.

Task 2: Analysis of the Community Safety Officer Program

Force field analysis assumes that energy is not created or destroyed but moved. We first describe one sign of the strengths of the program, and then name the problems. Our next step is to analyze these in the light of current adult learning theory.

Force Field Analysis

1.   At your table, describe one community volunteer who you see as a successful safety officer as a result of your training program. Brag about him or her! We'll hear a sample.

2.   Identify one serious problem you see in the training program. We'll hear and record all.

Task 3: How Adults Learn

1.   Describe at your table the best learning experience in your life. Analyze it by citing the factors that made it so good for you.

2.   Listen to this lecture about the factors named by Malcolm Knowles, adult educator, in his book *The Modern Practice of Adult Education* (1980).

3.   Compare your factors to Knowles's factors. What strikes you in terms of your training program with the community?

Task 4: How to Motivate Citizens

Kurt Lewin was a psychologist who worked on motivation for years at Cornell University. We have studied his book and offer you what we call *Lewin's dozen*, a set of principles of adult learning, to help you motivate the citizens you are training as safety officers.

1.   At your table, select one number. Read and study those principles, marking what you see as important.

2.   Share what you have learned by teaching your colleagues each principle you read. Begin at your table with principle 1 and go to 12. We'll share what you learned in the large group.

Task 5: Monologue and Dialogue

Paulo Freire is a Brazilian teacher who makes clear the distinction between giving people information (he calls this the "banking" approach) and offering them education (he calls this approach "problem-posing dialogue"). Jubilee calls these two processes *monologue* and *dialogue*, and you will have the opportunity here to experience and compare them.

1.   *Dialogue* Put the cards with the seven steps of planning on them into the order you as a table group agree is most useful when planning an educational event. When you have completed this ordering, go around and look at what people at the other tables have agreed on.

2.   *Monologue* Listen to the instructor's presentation of the seven steps of planning. Write down your questions or comments.

3.   *Differences between dialogue and monologue* At your table, identify the differences you felt between the experiences of monologue and dialogue.

Task 6: Generative Themes of a Community: Learning Needs Assessment

1.   Read the short handout that explains themes of a community. Identify some of the themes you have heard in this small learning community so far. We'll share a sample.

GENERATIVE THEMES

Generative themes are those ideas and issues, problems and joys, that people talk about, worry about, and celebrate!

A family whose house has been broken into will be jumpy and nervous. They hear noises at night. Their theme is "fear."

A grandmother will readily tell you about her generative theme: her new grandson!

A woman whose husband has lost his job will manifest her generative theme in the way she walks and in the look on her face. She is worried! She is depressed!

A student near examination time is nervous, talks quickly, is irritable at home, and finds himself drinking a lot. His generative theme is the exam!

Why "generative" themes? Why do you think it is important for you to know the themes of the community people you teach?

2.   When we are doing a learning needs assessment, we search for the generative themes of the learners so that we might address them in our design. Consider what you saw us do prior to this course: the survey, the telephone calls, our study of the training program, and our attendance at a program. What else might we have done? We'll share your ideas. Identify ways you can do a learning needs assessment in your training of citizen volunteers. We'll share a sample.

Task 7: Cognitive/Affective/Psychomotor Aspects of Learning

1.   Examine the symbol in Figure 9.1 and listen to the explanation provided.

All learning can use all three factors: cognitive (ideas), affective (feelings), and psychomotor (actions). As often as possible, we want to use activities that use as many of these factors as we can.

2.   How have you seen us try to use all three in this workshop so far?

3.   Read the following critical incident, which is a case study posing a problem. Decide at your table how Kate Farrell could use the three aspects of learning to enhance her teaching. What else can she use from what you have studied today about adult learning?

KATE FARRELL'S DILEMMA

Kate Farrell is an army nurse working in Haiti. She speaks French well since she grew up in New Orleans. She is in

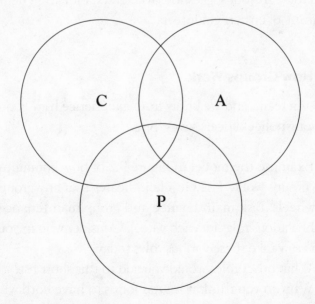

FIGURE 9.1. Three Aspects of Learning.

charge of a clinic where mothers come to receive food supplements for their children under five. She has been teaching a group of mothers about infant nutrition and the use of their babies' growth charts to monitor health and development.

The fifteen women she is working with clearly do not read or write. They have never been to school. Lieutenant Kate Farrell is telling them all that she learned about nutrition and using growth charts in her nursing school classes. But they do not seem to get it!

She thinks these Haitian mothers are all pretty stupid! Why can't they understand and demonstrate to her how they can feed their babies from all the food groups and how they can tell from the growth charts whether their child is doing well or not? Instead, they sit there like lumps, nodding respectfully, nursing their babies, not learning a thing! Lieutenant Farrell is frustrated.

4. How can your suggestions to Lieutenant Farrell help you in your training of citizen volunteers?

Task 8: How Groups Work

A group is a team, and we know from experience how good teamwork among police officers saves lives.

1. Examine the model in Figure 9.2 of how community and learning groups work. The bicycle indicates that any group works on two wheels: task maintenance and group maintenance. Now look at the various roles for each wheel. Consider who in your table group you saw take these various roles today.

2. What other roles would you add to this short list?

3. Why do you think it is vital for us to have both wheels in motion for any learning group?

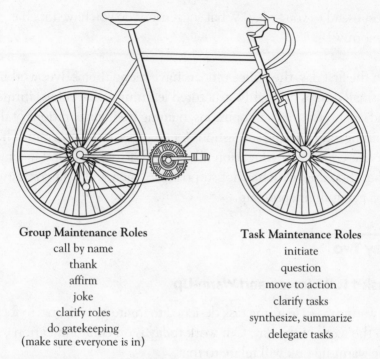

Group Maintenance Roles	Task Maintenance Roles
call by name	initiate
thank	question
affirm	move to action
joke	clarify tasks
clarify roles	synthesize, summarize
do gatekeeping	delegate tasks
(make sure everyone is in)	

FIGURE 9.2. How Groups Work.

Task 9: Review of Readings in *Learning to Listen, Learning to Teach*

1.   Select one chapter from *Learning to Listen, Learning to Teach* that tells a story that speaks to you personally. What strikes you about the story and its principle that you can use in your design of community education of citizen volunteers? Share with your table group. We'll hear a sample.

2.   Examine all the principles and practices we have used so far today. [These cards are on a chart, having been put up as they have been used during the day.] What are your questions? Which one seems most important to you?

Task 10: Evaluation and Closure of Day One

To evaluate day one, respond to the following questions: What was most useful to you today? What suggestions do you have for changes tomorrow?

On the first day, the police officers have found themselves working in small groups on highly structured learning tasks, being affirmed and celebrated for their opinions, naming their expectations of the training, and offering suggestions for changes in the program. They have used popular education all day and no doubt found it some-what shocking, which is not surprising of men and women trained in a paramilitary program.

Day Two

Task 11: Welcome and Warm-Up

A warm-up is a learning task designed to invite participants to focus on the work of the day. Our work today is on communications, so the warm-up task will relate to that.

1.   In pairs at your tables, describe where you were in 1986, what you were doing. Tell where you see yourself in 1996. Then tell where you hope to be in the year 2006. What strikes you about what you hear from the others at your table? We'll share a sample.

2.   Let's look at the program of the day. What are your questions?

Welcome, Warm-Up, Program Review

Communications Theory and Practice

Using a Video in Problem-Posing Adult Learning

Generative Themes of a Group

Open Questions

Demonstration of a Popular Education Design

Evaluation and Closure

Task 12: Communications Theory and Practice

1.   Listen to the following story:

THE LOST KEYS

My husband and I were having breakfast this morning and as he got up to go to work he discovered he had misplaced his keys. I was frustrated and said "Honestly! You are always losing those keys!" "Oh, honey, help me," he implored. "You know I have to be at this important meeting at the bank at nine." I grudgingly got up to help. "Oh thanks, honey," he said. As we both searched through the house, I remembered that we had been at the movies the night before and he had been wearing his raincoat. We both laughed as we headed for the closet together. There in the pocket were the car keys. "Thanks, my dear!" he said as he kissed me good-bye.

While it looks like there are two people in this story, they each take on some very different traits throughout it, don't they? Eric Berne, a Canadian psychologist, had a sense that we all move in and out of different ego states and that our communication with one another is affected by what ego state we are in.

2.   Read the following brief description of Berne's theory:

BERNE'S THEORY

Eric Berne, a Canadian doctor, had worked for years with Freud's approach to health and healing. One day he decided it was all too complicated and set out to make it simple enough for ordinary people to grasp.

Berne suggested that Freud's *superego, ego,* and *id* could be understood as basic states of being of the person—what he called *ego states.* He suggested that the superego can be seen as the *Parent ego state*, the id as the *Child ego state*, and the ego as the *Adult ego state.*

The Parent ego state has two forms: the *Critical Parent* and the *Nurturing Parent*. The Critical Parent scolds, admonishes, criticizes, and warns. The Nurturing Parent, in another voice, shows concern, warns in a loving way, and admonishes tenderly. As you can imagine, the Parent ego state, whether critical or nurturing, can hook the Child ego state in another.

The Child ego state also has two forms: the *Adapted Child*, who adapts his or her behavior to the demands of the Parent ego state in another, and the *Natural Child*, who shows a free, playful spirit.

Because each of us has had parents or parental figures in our lives, we each have a Parent ego state. Because each of us has been a child, we each have a Child ego state. And we all have a cool, thinking Adult ego state.

These ego states have nothing to do with age. From an early age, we all have the capacity to act differently at different times. Have you ever seen a three-year-old shake an angry finger at his brother, taking the same stance the father takes? The three-year-old is acting out of his Critical Parent ego state.

The Adult ego state is available to each of us: thinking, cool, reasoning, sensible. In a moment of conflict, for example, when one person in a Critical Parent ego state is shouting at another, and that other is responding in tears from an Adapted Child ego state, one of them may ask a simple question from the Adult ego state and thereby transform the situation!

Berne called such an encounter a transaction, and he named the science of understanding such encounters *transactional analysis*.

3.   Listen to this illustrated lecture about what you have just read. What are your questions?

4.   Describe in your table group one or more ego states you perceived yourself in since you woke this morning. We'll hear a sample.

5.   Identify verbs that you associate with each of the ego states.

6.   Name some uses of this communications theory in your work in community education of citizen volunteers.

Eric Berne's theory of communication presented in this manner has proven useful to students of popular education all over the world. This approach is essentially an effort to get into an Adult/Adult mode of communication, which Jubilee calls dialogue. In this challenging situation, with police officers used to a more command/obey approach (what Berne would call Parent/Child), this theory can be very helpful in explaining why dialogue is more effective in adult learning.

Task 13: Using a Video in Problem-Posing Adult Learning

1.   This video shows a physician teaching a group of women. The doctor has clearly never heard of popular education nor of the principles and practices we have been studying. She is teaching as she was often taught in medical school. While you look at this video, write down on these cards three things you might suggest she do to make her teaching more accountable. That is, what three things can she do to be more certain that the women are learning what they came to learn. We'll hear what each table group has to offer.

2.   What strikes you about how we used this video? For example: It was posing the problem of teaching via monologue. We set a learning task before the video was shown. What else?

Task 14: Open Questions

1.   What differences do you see between the following questions?

Do you like this workshop?

How can I help you?

What have you found is the best way to protect your
community?

What is your middle name?

What was the best session in this workshop for you?

How will you as a police officer use this new way of
teaching?

What for you is the difference between a closed and an open
question?

2. The following are closed questions. How can you make
them open questions? Change each one.

Do you like this workshop?

Is this a good setting for the workshop?

Would you prefer coffee or tea?

Do you know how to shoot a gun?

Are there any questions?

3. Design one open question you might use to invite dialogue
in a community group of citizen volunteers. Write that question on
a card and post it for all to share. We'll examine them all.

4. Consider this axiom: open questions invite dialogue. At
your table, tell what that might mean in your work with citizen
volunteers.

Task 15: Designing Together

We have examined the theory of popular education as it relates to
doing training of citizen volunteers from communities. We will now
attempt to design together a training of citizen volunteers.

The instructor leads this design working at a flip chart, inviting
input from participants.

AN INTRODUCTION TO COMMUNITY SAFETY TRAINING IN OAKDALE

1.   *Who?* A small group of concerned citizens has written to the police chief asking for two training officers to come to the community to introduce the citizen training course. They will announce this first session in the community and invite participation from their neighbors. What else should we know about those who are definitely coming to the first session? Men? Women? Ages? Work profile? How will we do a needs assessment of this group?

2.   *Why?* The community of Oakdale is interested in having a citizen volunteer safety corps. They need to know what kind of training is offered to citizens, about what, by whom, how long, when, where, and so forth. Many of them have said they would like to be trained to be safety officers. State legislation provides resources for such training.

3.   *When?* The session will last from 7:00 P.M. to 9:00 P.M. on Monday, March 7, enough time for six learning tasks at twenty minutes per task. How does this time fit the lifestyle of community members? How can we find that out?

4.   *Where?* The session will be held at the Oakdale community center. How can the room be arranged? How can participants work in small groups? Will there be child care if both parents want to attend? How much of this should be written into the design?

5.   *What?* The following is the content of the evening, the knowledge, skills, and attitudes to be modeled; what else do you see as essential to teach during the evening?

The experience of a citizen volunteer from a nearby community

The legislation that set up the program

Outline of the training course

Community-specific needs as to logistics of the course

The experience of each of the two training officers

6. *What For?* Following are the achievement-based objectives for this two-hour session; what else would you add to this set of achievement-based objectives for a two-hour course? At the end of this session, all participants will have:

Heard from a citizen volunteer from another community about his role and function in his own community

Reviewed the state legislation that set up the citizen safety program

Examined the training course outline

Identified their needs in relation to training course logistics

Met the training officers who will do their training course

7. *How?* Following are the learning tasks and materials for the evening:

TASK I: WELCOME, PROGRAM REVIEW, WARM-UP

1. *Welcome* Thank you for coming tonight. I am Jane, and this is my colleague Joan. We have designed a two-hour program for you tonight using the same process we will be using throughout the course. We are thankful for the collaboration of Mr. Smith, from this community, who spoke with us and gave us a tour of your neighborhood. Let me now review the achievement-based objectives on this chart, and the content on this other chart.

Expectations are not asked for in this session since the program is set for only two hours.

2. *Warm-Up* At your tables, decide on some reasons why Oakdale might find a community safety program useful at

this time. Write each reason on a card and post them here on this chart entitled "Why We Want a Community Safety Program Now." We will review all of them.

What else would you add to that task, or how would you change it?

TASK II: MEET A COMMUNITY SAFETY OFFICER

Before you meet Sam Jones, a community safety officer, write down at your table all the questions you have for him. Listen to Sam describe his role and function in Lawnwood Community where he lives.

Ask Sam the questions that still remain unanswered for you.

What other learning tasks would you want to set for the group around Sam Jones's talk?

TASK III: THE COMMUNITY SAFETY LEGISLATION

Read the following summary of the community safety law that was passed in this state in 1990. What are your questions?

At your table, discuss what you would say to Senator Goodman who sponsored this law. We'll hear from each table or a sample.

The purpose here is to have the citizens in this community comprehend that they have a right by law to this training. What else would you have them do with their reading of that law?

TASK IV: REVIEW OF THE TRAINING DESIGN AND PARTICIPANTS' SPECIFIC NEEDS

1. At your table, read the following topical outline of the six-week training course for citizen safety officers. Note the application form. The total hours in training are twenty-four hours a week. What are your questions?

Is there any other learning task you would suggest around this training course outline? The topical outline contains only the achievement-based objectives, the content, and the titles of the tasks on each night.

2. At your table, identify what you as a citizen would need to be able to complete this course. Write each need on a card and post the cards on the chart. We will read and address all needs you name as far as we can.

How can the citizens be helped to understand that the needs they named may not be met in a short course? The instructors invite learners to name their needs not in order to form the training program, but certainly to inform it. Knowing up front such information as there will not be day care for young children during the training course, that they will not be paid for their volunteer time as a safety officer, or that the state will provide insurance for them, builds the safety of the learning scene. When adult learners feel sure and safe, they can take the risks needed to learn.

TASK V: MEET THE TRAINING TEAM

Listen to the training officers tell why they enjoy their community training jobs, where they have already done it, and what they feel it has achieved. What are your questions to each officer?

The participants have been working with these officers all night. This is a time for them to hear from these police officers about themselves. What would you add to or change about this learning task?

TASK VI: EVALUATION AND CLOSURE

If you are interested in doing the training course that will begin on March 15th, please complete the application form in the training course materials you reviewed in Task 4. If you take the form home, you can send it to us. It has our address on the back.

At your tables, name one thing that was most useful for you tonight. Name also one thing you suggest be changed about this process. We'll hear from each table. Thank you!

The officers will have to record what they hear of this evaluation task.

Review the entire finished design that we just edited together. What are your questions about designing a training program using this popular education approach?

The exciting thing about this process is that the dialogue is captured as they design. As general agreement emerges for a change in the design, the facilitator adds that change to the program. Everyone reads what is being written as it is being added. Having gone through this process, the teams are ready to design for themselves.

Task 16: Evaluation and Closure

Lay out on your table all the principles and practices cards. What are your questions about any one of them? Which one seems most useful to you as you design community training for citizen volunteers? Which one seems irrelevant to this training work of the police department?

Day Three

Task 17: Welcome and Warm-Up

In your table groups, name what you feel uncertain or apprehensive about as you begin your designs. Listen to your colleagues' responses to your fears. We'll share a small sample of "what ifs" and responses.

Task 18: Design in Teams of Two

Select a partner and design a one-hour training session for community citizen volunteer safety officers. Teach them one part of the required curriculum, using all the principles and practices of popular education. Prepare problem-posing learning materials for your design. Use the instructors as resource people.

Task 19: Microteaching and Feedback

1. *Microteaching* Each team teaches one section of the required curriculum to their colleagues, who respond as potential citizen volunteers. This microteaching is videotaped and the team gets the opportunity to review their teaching before they go back to the drawing board.

2. *Feedback* The following questions are addressed to the team who did the teaching:

> What did you like about your design for citizen training and your teaching?
> What will you change next time in your design and in your teaching?

The following questions are addressed to the participants who were their learners:

> What did you like about this design?
> What suggestions do you offer the team for changes?

The teaching teams are not asked to defend their designs or teaching styles. When they hear suggestions for changes, their only role is to welcome these as suggestions. Whether or not they use them is entirely up to them.

Day Four

Task 20: Back to the Drawing Board

Select another section of the required training to use for your team's second microteaching. Design another one-hour session using all the feedback received from the first session.

Task 21: Second Microteaching and Feedback

Teach using your new design, which will also be videotaped for your reflection. The feedback session described in Task 19 is repeated, with particular reference this time to specific principles and practices.

Day Five

Task 22: Synthesis

In pairs, examine the synthesis questions [Task 10 in Chapter Two]. Select four that you feel you will find most useful in designing your work with community safety volunteers. Respond to them with your partner.

Task 23: Redesigning the Curriculum

In pairs, select two of those sections of the training curriculum that have not been used this week and design them using this popular education approach. As your designs are completed, present them via overhead projection to the group.

The instructor will now have a completely redesigned version of the traditional citizen volunteer training curriculum to give to the police chief. The redesign has been done by the training officers.

Task 24: Evaluation and Closure

1.   At your table, share what was the highlight of this workshop for you. We will hear all comments.

2.   Review the achievement-based objectives. What strikes you about what we accomplished?

3.   What do you see are your next steps in the process of community education?

Thank you!

This example of a training program for a group of police officers is offered with the hope that it will, in fact, be tried. It is also offered to demonstrate how context affects the structure and content of any training program.

10

Supporting Newly Trained Trainers

Strategies for Continuing Dialogue

Founding itself upon love, humility and faith, dialogue becomes a horizontal relationship of which mutual trust between the dialoguers is the logical consequence. It would be a contradiction in terms if dialogue—loving, humble and full of faith—did not produce this climate of mutual trust, which leads the dialoguers into ever closer partnership in the naming of the world.
—Paulo Freire (1993, p. 72)

An integral part of this educational service involves "after care." When individuals with years of teaching experience or training practice leave a five-day training course, they are novices in this new approach. I recognize that a short course, even a semester-long course at graduate school, including two practice efforts at design and teaching, cannot transform habits built up over years. What kind of support and follow-up is necessary to confirm their skills, to corroborate their new knowledge, and to celebrate new and healthier attitudes toward themselves, their colleagues, and the adult learners they will be teaching?

The Educator as Subject

I honor the fact that the adult educators who have explored a new way of teaching may not be willing or able to put it into practice in their training situation. They are always subjects (decision makers) in their own lives. Whether they use this approach or not is their decision. It must also be their decision to access resources for support and follow-up. The role of the trainers of trainers, the educators of educators, is to be available and accessible, and to make the resources as accessible as possible.

Educators using participative, problem-posing, accountable approaches to adult learning are swimming against the stream. Adult students themselves will show resistance to such a demanding approach, often because it is so unfamiliar. I recall a group of college professors in a small southern college complaining vigorously to me because they could not find the professor's place in the classroom I had arranged for our graduate course in adult education. We read in Chapter Three about the young Chilean physician who argued forcefully that he had not come to dialogue with his colleagues but to listen to Dr. Vella! A one-week course cannot prepare adult educators for all the initial resistance they may meet.

Resources

On the last day of Jubilee's five-day course, we share a list of currently known resources. Highlander Center in New Market, Tennessee has an incredible history of popular education events and efforts in the surrounding Appalachian counties. Their publications, newsletter, and courses are a rich resource. The Doris Marshall Institute in Toronto, Canada, is another popular education resource center, with publications and courses teaching community educators. We urge adult educators to subscribe to journals like *Convergence* that will share research efforts in this field. We ask them to put their name on the mailing list of publishers like Jossey-Bass who are continually creating new resources toward accountable learning. Jubilee's quarterly *News Notes* carries information on training events and new publications and resources. Membership in adult education professional organizations is encouraged. These organizations, like the North American Alliance for Popular and Adult Education, have professional journals and national conferences that sometimes feature this new approach. Jubilee has a useful review service frequently used by Jubilee Fellows. They fax us their designs for training, we review them, adding our suggestions for changes, and fax them right back, often the same day. This service offers a safety net for new trainers using popular education. They say, "I feel you are the other person on my design team when you respond like that!" Jubilee now responds to about three or four designs every week, and the number is growing.

Collaboration

Adult educators who have striven to transform their approach to learning need one another. We urge Jubilee Fellows—those who have completed the five-day course—to meet regularly and to share their designs with one another. Here the concept of competition needs to be examined. This word means asking (petition) with (com). We have to "ask with" one another, with colleagues who are in the same struggle, how we can teach more effectively, how we can design for dialogue. We need one another as allies, as editors, and as critics. My dear colleague Tom Sappington once said, "There is plenty of work to go around!" This is a new attitude that we at Jubilee hope to foster at every level within the course and afterwards.

Events

The second course is a structured opportunity for adult educators to meet to review their independent designs for training and adult learning. It is a two-day session for six educators at a time. It is a rich learning opportunity with a review of all the principles and practices done through the examination of new designs presented by participants.

We urge all who will use this approach to training trainers to set up such a second course or an ongoing seminar on popular education. A series of these can not only stimulate further learning in this approach to adult education but also correct misconceptions and clean up designs before they are used.

For example, Julia Beamish, who works at Family Health International, brought to a second course her tentative design for a training manual for journalists who might teach about family planning through their media. We worked on her design together and the result of our collaboration is a best-selling international resource entitled *Journalists Training Course in Family Planning*. Julia points to the feedback and constructive advice offered in the second course as the turning point in the production of that training program. I offer this example as an illustration of what can happen when there is adequate follow-up and support of adult educators after the introduction to popular education.

Refresher courses based on the generic model shown in Chapter Two can be useful, especially a few years after the initial training. Jubilee Fellows who come back to take the training course a second time marvel at how it has changed over the years. As research continues and as we improve our own efforts and materials, it is wise to offer the course again to those who have done it some years ago. Training organizations might give discounts to encourage adult educators to repeat the course after five years of working with the approach.

Fellowships

One training event that we have found fruitful and effective for educators of adults is the Fellowship, in which an educator works with a training specialist for two or three months. In Jubilee's system, Fellows are offered a substantive bibliography and spend a good deal of the time reading and researching adult education issues. They attend a one week-long training course during their Fellowship and assist in the design and teaching of any programs Jubilee is doing during that period. Such Fellowships could be offered at adult education departments of universities or colleges or through adult education centers similar to Jubilee. The richness in this approach is the quiet time for reflection, the engagement in actual training events, and the stimulating conversations with peers. Jubilee has an axiom that suggests there are three things that make effective adult education: time, time, and time! The advantage of a Fellowship is the time available to the learner for both action and reflection.

Cluster Meetings

In Raleigh, Boston, and Vermont there are cluster meetings of individuals who have studied popular education. The agenda involves sharing successes and problems with designs and trainings and reviewing new designs for feedback. It is a useful time when people can speak freely of their own learning and of their efforts to help others learn using the principles and practices of popular education. These clusters of Jubilee Fellows or other interested adult educators who bring their designs to be reviewed or who read and discuss a current book together can be a valuable resource. The informal structure builds personal strength as well as a bond of friendship and professional collaboration.

I called Tom Sappington one morning to ask if he were able to go to the Dominican Republic to offer a "paper" on this popular approach to a conference of the World Health Organization. He was delighted and asked if I could in turn do a workshop on leadership development with the directors of the Hospice of North Carolina in a mountain retreat in western North Carolina. So Tom went off to an international conference in Santo Domingo while I spent a quiet morning in the Blue Ridge Mountains. This kind of collaborative effort can only occur when we realize that we are not competing against one another, but asking with one another, "How can this learning best be accomplished?"

As you saw in Chapter Three, health professionals in Chile have formed a collaborating group who meet monthly to share their efforts at Educación Popular. In order to avoid becoming an exclusive club, each doctor or nurse who has done the training course brings one interested colleague to each meeting. In 1995 a second course was provided for the original participants and Jubilee will offer another five-day training to a new group of community physicians and nurses in 1996. These subsequent programs are an illustration of concern not only for follow-up but also for expansion.

Congruence

In the effort to be of service to adult educators after they have done a train-the-trainers course, it is important to be cautious so as not to refer them to programs that are not congruent with the approach they have learned. There are adult education courses, as we all know, that do not honor the principles and practices reviewed in this book. There is an academic, hierarchical approach to adult education that looks very much like what we all have experienced at one time or another in school. Jubilee does not want to grow into an organization of professionals who read learned papers at one another in defiance of all we have struggled to learn and teach.

Electronic Communication

More and more people are only a moment away from one another via modem. How can an electronic communication system be developed locally to support and follow-up with one another after the training course? This is an unexplored arena, waiting for creative thinking and deliberate effort. One example of such creativity is an international network. The San Francisco Bay Area Popular Education group in collaboration with North American Popular Educators and the North American Alliance for Popular and Adult Education is cohosting an electronic conference on Popular Education on the Association for Progressive Communications (APC) global networks. The access code is <edu.popular>. The network in the United States is the Institute for Global Communications (IGC); the network in Canada is Web. The power of dialogue can be enhanced by technology!

Universities and colleges have alumni associations to serve their graduates with ongoing programs and networking opportunities. What can organizers of train-the-trainers courses offer to those who take their courses to assure them that they are valuable associates and that the ongoing development of their skills and knowledge is vital? This is an important research agenda for all who educate adult educators and train trainers, and this chapter has suggested some basic approaches. This kind of learning, however, is never over. There is no end to the need for support and dialogue.

11

Evaluation

Beginning to Assess the Results

One cannot expect positive results from an educational or political action program which fails to respect the particular view of the world held by the people. . . . The starting point for organizing the program content of education or political action must be the present, existential, concrete situation, reflecting the aspirations of the people. We must pose this existential, concrete present situation to the people as a problem which challenges them and requires a response—not just at the intellectual level, but at the level of action.

—Paulo Freire, 1993, pp. 76–77

In *Learning to Listen, Learning to Teach* (1994), I introduced twelve specific principles and practices used in popular education to design for dialogue, to listen to learners, and to move to accountable learning. This book has examined more principles and practices that work in teaching adults how to teach other adults by using popular education approaches. My next book will be on the process of evaluation: How can the results of training that uses the popular approach methods be effectively and cogently measured?

Paulo Freire has spoken eloquently of the need to measure success by action in the oppressive situation that was the catalyst of an educational event. If we are addressing the problems faced by teachers of adults, for example, the only significant evaluation indicator is a notable reduction in those problems. The key is to look for action indicators. For example, if adult students do not come back to courses, if they drop out and disappear, that is a critical problem. When teachers use popular education methods and see adult learners engaged, interested, and excited about their own learning and development and coming back faithfully to classes, those are action indicators of the success of train-the-trainers programs. In industry, the cost of retraining staff is very high. When adult learners learn accountably on the first course and do not need to come back for retraining in the same skill, that is an action indicator. There is qualitative evidence of competence and confidence when factory or office workers offer to teach their colleagues what they learned, and there is quantitative evidence when there is measurable cost saving.

Quantitative results such as test scores do not tell the story in the evaluation of adult learning. Tests are instruments from formal, traditional learning systems. Even when teaching the Myers-Briggs Type Indicators in staff development seminars, I assiduously avoid the use of the very word "test." The Myers-Briggs instrument is not a test; however, if adults see it as such, they necessarily assume one response is better than another. The question is visible on every face: What is the right answer? What do I have to do to score high on this test?

Adults who are learning skills to advance their careers or to do their job more efficiently, more quickly, and more competently want to see action indicators, not test scores. They want to go back to their work station knowing that they know what they know because they just did what they were learning and have received feedback and affirmation.

Adults learning about AIDS or STDs, for example, must have action indicators in their own lives that show them they can be safe. When learning is a matter of life and death, a test score offers little consolation. In my next book, I will invite readers to examine ways to quantify action indicators that show adults as more competent, more confident, and more likely to share their new learning. Such qualitative indicators—human signs—speak to the success or failure of adult learning efforts.

An Action Indicator Using a Checklist of Competencies

One action indicator of the success of a training course in popular education is the regular use of the following comprehensive checklist of competencies. When trainers respond to all these questions, they are intentional about how they use the principles and practices.

Checklist of Competencies
Toward Effective Designs in Popular Education

Have you

1. Been in dialogue with adult students prior to the course?
   Yes____ Not yet____

2. Prepared the course by using all seven steps of planning?
   Yes____ Not yet____

3. Negotiated the size of the group of optimal learning?
   Yes____ Not yet____

4. Set learning tasks for small groups of learners to teach the content? Yes____ Not yet____

5. Examined these learning tasks for sequence: easy to more difficult, simple to complex? Yes____ Not yet____

6. Designed a warm-up as learning Task 1 that is related to the topic and appropriate for the group? Yes____ Not yet____

7. Honored in your design the fact that adult learners are subjects of their own lives? Yes____ Not yet____

8. Named content (skills, knowledge, and attitudes) clearly and cogently? Yes____ Not yet____

9. Designed achievement-based objectives that can be readily evaluated? Yes____ Not yet____

10. Selected a site that lends itself to small-group work?
    Yes____ Not yet____

11. Kept an eye on the time frame so that learning tasks can be accomplished, avoiding too much "what" for the "when"? Yes___ Not yet___

12. Used open questions to stimulate dialogue throughout? Yes___ Not yet___

13. Examine each learning task for its cognitive, psychomotor, and affective potential? Yes___ Not yet___

14. Designed for safety of teacher and learners? Yes___ Not yet___

15. Set up processes and structures (small groups, breaks, gallery walk review of charts) to assure inclusion? Yes___ Not yet___

16. Used brainstorming or associative processes without judging or editing? Yes___ Not yet___

17. Designed for optimal engagement of all via small group work, learning tasks, affirming responses, echoing? Yes___ Not yet___

18. Avoided monologue by designing for dialogue? Yes___ Not yet___

19. Designed a synthesis learning task to summarize all that has been learned? Yes___ Not yet___

20. Designed in quiet, reflective time for learners to think about what they are learning? Yes___ Not yet___

21. Designed adequate closure tasks? Yes___ Not yet___

22. Designed an opportunity for small groups to examine their own group and task maintenance? Yes___ Not yet___

23. Used a wide variety of techniques? Yes___ Not yet___

    Brainstorming via snow cards

    Critical incident and open questions

    Echoing or paraphrasing

    Lavish affirmation

Lecture that is not monologue but part of the learning task

Song, dance, mime, artwork

Found objects

Gallery walk for review

Handouts, summary notes

Stories

A Final Word

In my yellow kayak on a quiet lake I wrote this short verse:

> More's the miracle for me
> Not to walk on water
> But to sit on it.

If this book has kept your attention and has invited you to sit quietly to reflect on the processes of popular education, it has done its job. We'll walk on water later! I write not to convince, but to celebrate the wonders of both what we already know about adult learning and the immensity we have yet to discover. I thank you for sharing this celebration of the power of dialogue with me.

Resource

A Glossary of Concepts from Popular Education

This glossary describes and defines terms used throughout the book—the principles and practices of popular education as Jubilee understands and teaches them. It can be read as a reference, or as an additional chapter. I trust it will start some critical thinking on the meaning of these concepts.

Accountability: Who Is Accountable to Whom?

First, adult learners are clearly accountable to themselves. No teacher can learn for a learner. All learning is idiosyncratic, that is, each learner learns what he is ready and able to learn. Educators of adults must do all they can to be accountable to learners by carefully selecting people for courses, conducting adequate needs assessments, preparing achievement-based objectives, and designing feasible learning programs. They are accountable for ensuring that all learning materials are accessible, culturally and educationally appropriate, and useful. Educators are not, however, accountable for the learning that takes place among adults. This is hard truth to hear. Moore (1992) suggests that for a psychiatrist, "the urge to heal can get in the way of seeing." In an analogous manner, the urge to teach can get in the way of learning. Insofar as educators respect each adult learner as the subject of the learner's own life and learning, that is, as decision maker, they honor the diversity of the learning styles in a group.

In a situation in the Maldive Islands, during a ten-day training course, I was suddenly made aware that the work Jubilee had planned for the day was not going to fit the needs of the learners. These adult learners had persevered through six days and were manifestly tired of their classroom learning tasks. Since they were to work in the nearby villages that afternoon, we had a viable alternative. The instructors called a rather sudden break and changed the day's program, to everyone's advantage. We were thus accountable to the learners, not covering the curriculum in spite of them. We had listened to their unspoken learning needs and honored their autonomy.

If people are in fact not learning what their instructors are teaching, the instructors must examine their own accountability to the design and to the teaching process. Here is a place to hold together the opposites: accountability to the learners and their accountability to themselves. Paradoxically, accountability goes hand in hand with a certain detachment from the result of the affair. I have discovered that my own careful accountability—preparation, needs assessment, design, careful facilitation and listening, and evaluation and follow-up—almost always shows me that adults have learned a great deal more than I hoped to teach. The six diverse examples in Chapters Three through Eight demonstrate how accountability is an operative factor in the attitude of both teachers and learners, and how detachment is in fact the other operative side of the coin.

Affirmation: How Do Instructors Make Respect Felt?

Lavish affirmation is both a principle and a practice. Jubilee has discovered that it does not hurt adults to hear simple encouragement of their efforts: Well done! Good question! Yes! Very interesting! Hearing such praise almost always moves them to do more and better. What is encouraged here is the learning, not the product. Sometimes that learning effort is magnificent; sometimes it is pedestrian. It is always an effort and always deserves encouragement.

Why lavish? The danger of the infamous "plop" is ever present. A plop occurs when an adult learner responds to a question or asks a question or ventures an opinion and the instructor's response is a blank stare or silence or a move to the next task without reference to what the person said. Such a response is insulting, damaging, and destructive of learning. Let it happen once and the learner may not come back. Let it happen twice to the same person and you can be sure that learner will not come back.

Teachers are often absorbed in their content, concerned about "covering" what they think the learners need to know, anxious about time. They fall unwittingly into the "plop." Intention is not the issue here. When the learner has been so treated, the result is sure, no matter why the "plop" occurred. At a university staff retreat, a young professor, somewhat naive, told her male colleagues that she was grateful for the retreat time to share with them her feelings about education. She said she had been so busy all year driving around the state in her extension education job that she had had no time to get to know the others in the department. A serious, somewhat dour professor immediately responded: "Speaking of traveling, we have not been filling out the proper forms for the department cars." This plop drove the young professor to another university. How could those professors have affirmed that young woman and avoided the plop? How can teachers be taught to avoid the plop and affirm the efforts of their adult learners? Instructors in these train-the-trainers courses are bound to model awareness and avoidance of the plop.

Lavish affirmation means generous encouragement, clear and loud recognition of the effort an adult is making to learn new knowledge, skills, and attitudes. It is strikingly effective in motivating men and women to work hard at the hard work of learning.

Analysis: Can You Tell Why?

Interpreting Freire's problem-posing approach, Ira Shor (1980) suggests a slow waltz of learning activities: describe, analyze, and reconstruct. The moment of analysis is the moment of heightened learning in this three-step process. As instructors present new theory to adult learners, they describe it, then invite the learners to analyze it. They ask questions like, What's missing here? What does not seem right to you? What seems unnecessary? What seems incongruent? How can this be useful to you? These and other analytical open questions move the learners to analyze hypotheses (theories) presented and make them their own. When the learners, as Subjects of their own learning, work thus with new concepts, it is not only they who will change through the learning but the concepts themselves that will be affected by these new perceptions.

What are some analytical questions that can be put to a group of adult learners as they learn a skill? Here are a few examples: When will this skill be useful to you? How could you teach this to a child? How could you do this with fewer motions? What other instruments could you use besides those just demonstrated? What have you been doing all your life without this skill?

The purpose of analysis is not to transform the concept, skill, or attitude, but to invite the kind of critical thinking that can bring about a learning transformation in the adult. The consequent transformation of skills, knowledge, and attitudes is done by adult learners as they learn, as they decide what significance the theories and skills have in their own personal context. This principle/practice is deeply related to sequence and subject and the difference between a deliberative and consultative vote, and of course, to dialogue, the heart of the learning process.

The reconstruction Shor calls for is the creation of a new hypothesis. The new hypothesis may, however, be the very same hypothesis, enhanced, rather than amended, by the new perceptions. In a Jubilee-run session, as we taught a small hospice group the meaning of "stakeholders" in strategic planning (those who have a stake in the success of an enterprise), the nurses, social workers, chaplain, and administrator moved that concept to a new community plane as they identified the numerous stakeholders in the success of the community hospice and clustered those stakeholders into groups with similar stakes. They soon had a demographic, sociological profile of their small North Carolina town, and of the entire state in that all the stakeholders in the work of the hospice were widely distributed. The concept of stakeholder has never been the same for me.

Aspects of Learning: Ideas, Feelings, Actions

When learning, human beings can use three faculties: the mind, to consider ideas or cognitive material; the heart, the affective faculty, or feelings; and the muscles, in psychomotor activities. Popular education stresses that the most effective learning uses all three aspects of learning as often as possible.

The history of formal human learning is largely cognitive. This is why information is often mistaken for education. The adult learner, not unlike the waking child, is able to use heart, head, and hands to learn. The educator's job is to design opportunities to use all three.

Autonomy: Who Is It Who Will Tell Me Who I Am?

I see the purpose of all education to be the development of personal autonomy. This is not achieved by wishful thinking, but by learners practicing personal autonomy in every learning task. Working in small groups does not lessen personal autonomy. It can build it through the natural give and take that occurs in that setting.

When individual adult learners question the content and argue about the skills and attitudes being taught, the educator has a responsibility to honor their perspective and welcome their honest response. This is not always easy. If you can recognize indicators of autonomous behavior and celebrate them, you can use these as steps on the way to the adult learner's success. I offer an axiom: if you are not disputing it, you are not learning it.

Often, signs of autonomy are seen as rebellion or disrespect to the teacher. If the design invites such signs from the adult learners, a defensive reaction from the teacher can be avoided. Disagreement and questioning are desirable. The learning tasks discussed in this book invite that behavior in order to develop a questioning attitude. Lavish affirmation can be offered when such signs are observed in training programs. Such affirmation encourages adult learners to use their autonomy as a way to do critical thinking about what they are learning. Educators have tended to suspect that autonomy will lead to anarchy. This has not been my experience. Autonomy is a necessary condition for democracy, and democracy is not anarchy. The conditions and rules of the road for a learning event do not get dissolved by individuals acting as autonomous adults. This principle works harmoniously with the practice of small group work, in a strangely paradoxical manner. The more autonomous and mature the adult learner, the better the communication that takes place within the small learning group.

As you saw in Chapter Two, people are invited to work in pairs during the training course to design a microteaching event. They are asked to teach the entire group something they will be teaching other adults in their workaday world. On one occasion, two teams were going to do the same teaching. They expressed their concern about this as being repetitious for the group. I assured them that their autonomy, their own unique styles and treatment of the issues, would make each presentation different. It did. Autonomy, I realized, is the basis of the fact that all learning (and teaching) is idiosyncratic.

Case Studies: Short Stories with an Angle

A case study is a short story that poses a problem on the theme being studied. Jubilee's favorite story, of village nurse Kate Farrell, presented several times in this book (see Chapters Two, Three—in which she is known as Eliana Ferrer—Four, Seven, and Nine), takes on a life of its own in popular education training courses, as learners constantly refer to it while learning new concepts and skills: "Kate Farrell could have used this!" The affective aspect of the case study is vital. It must be a story distant enough to be safe and close enough to be immediate, presenting problems that are not impossible to resolve but that are serious enough to spend time on. Case studies are best kept short, and directly, clearly related to the issue at hand. Kate Farrell's story is a good one because she so obviously needs to learn the principles and practices of popular education. Using the problem-posing story to teach adult learners is truly education, inviting critical thinking.

The case study is a way to invite dialogue, through which people learn and test new theories. It is a way to do inductive learning, beginning with the particular incident, then applying the theory. Films, video clips, critical incidents (a small, highly focused case study), pictures, newspaper articles, photographs, and maps can all be used along with the case study or as a way to tell the story. The learning takes place as the participants work through the situation as it is presented, to apply the theory they know or to invite new theory.

Charts: Less Is More!

Using visual aids well is a skill that definitely is needed in this approach to adult learning, which honors the fact that adult learners retain twice as much if they have visual support.

Here is another Jubilee axiom: do not write on a chart what you will not use again. That is, do not use flip charts to record a dialogue or to keep records of a session. Do not put on a flip chart anything that will not be used by the entire group. This saves hundreds of thousands of trees, and keeps down what some call "psychological noise." When there are twenty different flip charts on the wall, the eye is drawn in many directions, the brain is askew, and the "noise" can be intolerable. Even if there is a need to use many flip charts, try to have only one on the easel at a time. This keeps the attention of adult learners focused and their minds clear.

Also, put all learning tasks on a flip chart in large, dark letters, even if the learning task is in the program booklet in front of learners.

Have you ever set a task and heard the participants mutter: "What is it we are supposed to be doing?" A central, clear, large chart with the learning task written on it takes care of that.

What colors work on flip charts? Dark blue, black, dark red, or dark green are best. Do not use orange or yellow or pink or other light colors, except as highlighters. This seems somewhat obvious, but my experience with trainers is that it does not hurt to say all this. These are technical points that seem small, but they have very important consequences when not observed. I advise teachers to examine billboards for techniques on charting. Fewer words are better than more, and the larger the print, the easier it is to read. Contrasting colors or sizes help to make the message clear. *Snow cards* are another way of charting, especially during brainstorming. Invite adult learners to write their thoughts on three-by-five white (snow) cards, one idea per card, and put those cards on a flip chart. The advantage of snow cards is their obvious mobility: you can move them about, cluster them, and put them in priority order, as needed. Post-it notes serve well as snow cards since they come ready to stick!

A *web chart* is a way of showing relationships between concepts. The theme of the chart is written in a circle in the center of the chart and the many diverse ideas are written to surround that circle. These ideas are then connected to one another, showing relationships and priorities. Jubilee has used such a chart to explore the concept of respect, putting that word at the center of the chart, and around it writing actions that show respect: calling people by name, listening, using appropriate cultural signs, affirming, echoing, thanking. The learners' ideas are circled and connected to one another and to the central theme. A web chart is a mirror of connections.

Closure: Where Have We Been? Where Do We Go from Here?

So much of good adult education is like good theater—carefully designed, intentional, and persuasive. It is vital to consider the

ending of a session and to make it as useful as possible in the corroboration of the participants' learning. Closure refers to those
activities that bring a session to a graceful ending, that synthesize
the content of learning, that review new skills, that preview upcoming sessions, and that thank participants for their efforts. Closure is
all too often neglected in adult learning. This neglect harks back to
formal classroom situations in which a bell marked the end of a
forty-five minute 'period' and the students jumped up, released at
last! It is clear how inappropriate that system is in training and
adult education programs, but it is in our blood.

The principle and practice of closure is a reminder to bring any
session, long or short, to a graceful ending. It is important to design
closure, to build in a task for it. Examples of such closure tasks are
manifest throughout the book.

Congruence: What I Say, I Do!

Nothing is more important than the behavior of the teacher, since
the learner, no matter what his or her age, is learning how to
behave from the teacher's example. The teamwork of instructors
will be reflected in the ways the participants' teams work in their
microteaching and evaluation; instructors' respectful listening to
all learners will be reflected in the learners' attitudes toward their
learners. The challenge to every adult educator is to do what they
are teaching. When leading a training course, I invite learners to
help me by saying at the outset of a learning event, "Look, I want
to model all these principles and practices we are going to learn,
but I know I will not do it perfectly. Help me by asking, when you
see something that looks incongruent, 'What's going on? Why did
you do that?'" The principle of congruence keeps the teacher's
teaching clean.

I offered this opening address about congruence to a graduate
school class once at the beginning of term. The young men and
women stared at me, uncomprehending and somewhat suspicious.
It was four weeks into the term before a daring young woman asked,

after a rather curt response I offered to a query, "Jane, could you not have shown more respect in your response? Could you not have said . . ." I had to sit down in awe at her acceptance of the challenge I had set. I said simply, "Ladies and gentlemen, start your engines. Now we can begin this course!" Four weeks was not too long to wait for the "death of the professor."

Consultative/Deliberative Votes: Suggest or Decide?

Participative popular education is a delicate balance between hearing the suggestions of learners and inviting them to make decisions about their own learning. It is never a case of all decisions being made by the learners or by the educator. It is a case of knowing what can be done by whom. When one gives a suggestion, it is a *consultative vote*. You can speak your heart, say what you feel, knowing it is only a suggestion. Conversely, when you make a decision, you are using a *deliberative vote*.

I was once at a very important learning event designed for professionals. The leader, a renowned psychologist, told the hundred or more participants to decide what they wanted to learn during the ten-day session. You can imagine the chaos that ensued. He was asking adult learners to take a deliberative vote when in fact they had none. He could have invited our consultative votes, examined our expectations and hopes and fears, then decided what could be done in the time allotted. He clearly did not understand the difference.

When preparing for a training session, the needs assessment and invitation to name expectations elicit consultative votes, suggestions. When learners decide what they will do for their practice teaching, they have a deliberative vote, and the instructors offer suggestions. It is important to know this difference, and not to confuse the two.

Design: Form Follows Function

What is generally called a lesson plan is what I now call a *design for adult learning*. The semantic difference is important: design involves a great deal of planning and the recognition of any number of aspects: Who is the design for? What is the situation that calls for such training? Where will it take place? What kind of time frame is available? What are the achievement-based objectives? What content (skills, knowledge, and attitudes) will be learned? How will everything be accomplished, and then evaluated? The response to all these questions—what Jubilee calls "the seven steps of planning"—is a design.

Design involves particular learning materials, selected media: video and audio presentations, flip charts, overhead projections, and handouts. When the design is complete, it will be a reliable podium for the educator to rest on. The safety of the educator is as important in adult learning as the safety of the learners.

The design ultimately is a set of learning tasks for the learners to do. This is always a delicate and difficult realization. Often, educators plan a lesson telling themselves what *they* will do, not what the learners will do. In the approach to adult learning presented in this book, the design indicates what the learner's learning tasks are.

An example of a learning task would be: "Examine this map of Raleigh with the health centers for senior citizens marked on it. Circle those nearest to your homes. What are your questions? Where would you tell a senior colleague to go for cardiovascular screening?" This is not a teaching task, but a learning task. As part of the design, participants are to respond to these in their learning groups by doing learning tasks. If the task were: "Tell the group where the health resources for senior citizens are in this town. Show them a map with the centers marked on it," it would be a teaching task.

When the design is inappropriate, adult learners will say so. This is a rewarding response that indicates their autonomy and feeling of safety. In a course introducing health education professionals to the principles and practices of adult learning, I had included a session on grant writing. They soon realized that the time they could spend on the course would not allow them to do a responsible job and they asked me to drop out the section on grant writing. I reluctantly agreed to do so. I wanted them to learn this skill, but

the design did not work for them. In this case, they had the deliberative voice.

The design of adult learning is difficult to develop. It is always
growing. The principles and practices discussed in this book can be
a guide to a wholesome, healthy design. The only real test, however,
is in the operation. If at the end of a session the participants know
that they know, your design worked!

Dialogue: Dia-Logos, The Word Between Us

This is the heart of the matter. Dialogue assumes two human beings
as subjects of their own learning, sharing research data, experience,
and questions to transform both their own learning and the very
knowledge they are examining. Paulo Freire says, "Dialogue is an
encounter between men mediated by the world in order to name
the world" (Freire, 1993, p. 69). Dialogue is the heart of popular
education, the reason why respect, honoring others as subjects of
their own learning, learning tasks, design, and all the rest of the
principles and practices are important. For teachers it is vital to
remember that it is in the dialogue that learning takes place.

Echoing: Say It Again, Sam!

Echoing, repeating, or paraphrasing what another person has said is
a way to affirm the person, to indicate that you are indeed listening
and that you have heard what was said, and to move the dialogue
into another phase. As part of a learning task, an instructor might
ask, "Which area do you think most needs the services of lawyers in
this large urban setting?" The group might respond, "The densely
populated slum area." Echoing this you say, "One area that needs
the services of lawyers is the slum area, which is densely populated.
Why do you believe this?" The dialogue goes on, based on the statement of perception. The learners know that the instructor has
heard them, and that all the others in the room have heard them.
The instructor knows that she or he has heard the learners correctly

because they do not try to correct the instructor's paraphrase of their position.

Echoing avoids crippling assumptions that lead people to say, "But I thought you said . . ." or "I heard you say. . . ." Echoing avoids the loss of time and focus that occurs when two groups move on to talk about two very different issues. When the instructor fails to echo the dialogue can get sidetracked. Once in a heated dialogue on the advantages and disadvantages of a union at the workplace of not-for-profit organizations, a small group began a discussion of the history of their organization. I was able, via the use of echoing, to respectfully point out that their dialogue was inappropriate and irrelevant to the issue at hand. Echoing is respectful, as the speakers are confirmed in what they said, because you were listening.

This is one of the skills of adult educators that manifest their ability to listen and their willingness to enter into a dialogue. The fatal plop referred to in the discussion of lavish affirmation can take place when the instructor forgets to echo responses to learning tasks.

Once in a training course I thought I heard a senior participant say he did not agree with one of the principles of learning set out by Kurt Lewin. When I paraphrased his statement I discovered that I had not heard it correctly. He not only agreed with Lewin, but he also had a few good examples of the application of the principle. If I had not echoed his words, I might have moved along and everyone would have missed his examples.

Energy: The Dynamism Created by Learning

A major part of the educator's job is to keep up the energy of the group of adult learners. Learning takes energy; it also makes energy. As people participate with vigor and enthusiasm in learning tasks that are relevant and have immediate usefulness to them, their energy rises. The work of the design is to evoke the energy that is in the group and use it to the learners' advantage.

In Tanzania, I designed and led leadership training courses for village men and women. We had to schedule the workshops into the middle of the day, when people could not work in the fields because of the hot sun. We worked in a relatively cool, thatched hut to which a dozen or so village leaders would come directly from their afternoon siesta. They were a sleepy crowd! As soon as we got them into learning tasks, however, the energy level in the room changed dramatically. The drowsy crowd became a lively set of learning groups, working over a relevant, meaningful task with growing energy. The decibel level in the mud and wattle hut rose, indicating their engagement.

I therefore see energy as a principle of adult learning: design to evoke the energy that is in the group by using all of the principles and practices.

A term often heard these days is "education for empowerment." I feel that power is in the adult learners even before they come to the training courses. It is the educator's job to design the learning event to enable the participants to know they have that power because they are using it, and then to celebrate with them the energy they demonstrate as they use their power. Educators do not put power in; they draw power out. It would be more accurate to speak of *ex*powerment than empowerment.

When energy in a group of adult learners is low, because of the hour or their natural fatigue, it is vital for the educator to recognize that and do something to get it up. Take a break, invite them to go out for a short walk, take an early lunch. Be aware of the energy level and of your responsibility to keep it high. Energy levels can be high while the group is quiet and reflective, as well as when they are actively engaged in more physical work.

Engagement: Without Engagement, There Is No Learning!

In 1951, Lewin taught that people learn more when they are involved in the learning, doing what they are learning, than when they are merely listening to someone talk about it. The engagement of learners is not only an indication that they are learning, it is how they learn. Knowles's (1980) research showed that adults learn 20 percent of what we hear, 40 percent of what we both hear and see, and 80 percent of what we do or discover for ourselves. Knowles was corroborating Lewin's discoveries, and he was also corroborating another famous teacher, Socrates, whose peripatetic school involved a walking dialogue. People learn critical thinking by doing critical thinking; they learn a new value system by working within it and testing it in their own situation. For example, computer skills are learned while working them out at the keyboard.

It seems clear that such involvement and engagement is possible with skills and attitudes, but how can theory engage learners? Paulo Freire helps with this by showing how all theory, all hypotheses, can be presented as an open system, posed as a problem for inquiry, reflection, and reconstruction. This approach is called *praxis*. The purpose of praxis is not only to create a new situation, but also to inspire intense action of the mind and the soul, as learners stretch their conceptual horizons and build new theories for themselves. During a graduate course at the School of Public Health at the University of North Carolina (UNC), Chapel Hill, the head of the department looked in one afternoon as the small groups were working intensely on some epistemological problem or other. "Why are they always so excited?" he inquired. "I think, Jim, it is because they are learning," I replied. Without engagement, there is no learning.

The train-the-trainers course must model teaching and learning by engagement, presenting theory and inviting adult learners to do something with it, demonstrating skills and attitudes and immediately inviting practice of those skills and attitudes.

Evaluation: How Do They Know That They Know?

Two forms of evaluation are used in the approach demonstrated in this book: immediate and long term.

Immediate evaluation is a response from adult learners in relation to the achievement-based objectives of the course. Where are they in terms of what the design said they would be learning and accomplishing? Immediate evaluation is done both daily and at the end of the course. *Formative evaluation* is the daily response; it forms and informs decisions about what to do the next day and how to do it. *Summative evaluation* is what occurs at the end of the program, when the participants' response sums up how well they feel the objectives have been achieved. Summative evaluation is also formative—of the next course.

The operative question is, how do they know they know? If adult learners are being approached as subjects of their own learning and development, the deliberative voice on evaluation is theirs. Only they can determine what they are learning. All learning is idiosyncratic, and our efforts to meet the needs of a group of twelve adults will necessarily have differentiated results. At the same time, there is a standard of achievement that the entire group must reach in order for the educators to know they have done their job. This is a case of "holding the opposites." Two kinds of evidence are needed: evidence of individual achievement and learning, and evidence of the group's moving toward goals set at the outset of the course. This is not an easy balancing act.

In the training course in a Latin American setting, the Save the Children community development project secretary was a participant because the SCF director wanted the whole team to learn this new approach to community education. Physicians, nurses, social workers, agronomists, and administrators in the project were moving quickly through the first tasks of the course, and it was clear that the young secretary was having some difficulty with both concepts and skills. People in her small task group came to me to protest that she was "holding them back." They were evaluating her progress for her. I spoke to her and she replied with enthusiasm about what she was struggling to learn. As she said, "This is new for me, and somewhat difficult. But I am learning so much so fast from my colleagues in my small group." I reported this to those colleagues, who thus discovered their own potential for both teaching and learning. We agreed to address the problem together at their table, and I heard the professionals celebrate her achievement and her wisdom in staying with this difficult learning task, and doing so well as a team member! I celebrated their change of heart, and they too knew that they had learned something more than what was being taught in the course: how to work together with diverse partners and make the experience valuable to everyone.

Effective evaluation means looking for clear, precise indicators. Indicators of success in the learning of skills, knowledge, and attitudes should be set up at the outset, in the design of a course. When responding to the "how" question in the seven steps of planning, learning tasks, materials, and evaluation indicators should all be included. Indicators can be new, consistent behaviors; creative, integrated expressions of new content; the solution of problem situations using new content and skills; or the use of new skills and the welcoming of feedback. Questions about the new content are also indicators, in that such questions and disputes show that the new content has been understood. Jubilee's axiom in this case is: if you cannot dispute it, you do not know it!

Indicators of behavioral change (in skills and attitudes) and of conceptual changes (in knowledge) can be as diverse as the adult learners themselves. However, it is imperative that some set of standard indicators be reached to assure that the achievement-based objectives have been accomplished. Indicators can be specific behaviors manifesting new skills, for example, using a software package, typing at a certain rate per minute, speaking clearly in a new language, or parallel parking a certain distance from the curb. Indicators can be consistent behavior over time manifesting a new attitude, for instance, self-confident questioning of a new concept, speaking in a group, letting others speak before jumping in on a conversation, or thanking others for their contribution.

Indicators can manifest new concepts at work. The use of certain language, using a set of newly learned guidelines when doing a job, inviting feedback in small group work as a function of what was learned about group and task maintenance are all indicators of newly grasped concepts. New concepts do not exist in isolation in adult learners. An objective test may indeed point out that an adult learner still does not know the capital of Utah; however, his or her experience with minority colleagues may be changed as a function of the concepts he learned while studying the history of the Mormon settlement in that state.

These are all immediate indicators, of recent learning. There are long-term indicators as well. For example, participants in Jubilee courses send their designs to us for review; they question some of the hypotheses; they develop learning materials and write books for educators using these principles and practices; they call Jubilee to work with their colleagues in further training. Long-term indicators do not always show that people accept what they have learned and use it. It is a reason for celebration when a Jubilee Fellow questions a basic premise, indicates how it has not worked for her, and suggests alternatives.

When organizations learn to do strategic planning together and to think strategically, their next projects, their new buildings, and their new hires are long-term indicators of success. In Tanzania, I taught for many years at a girls secondary school. The other teachers and I always said that the real evaluation of our teaching in that culture was, "What kind of grandmothers would these young women be?"

Expectations: What Do You Hope Will Happen?

Inviting adult learners to name their expectations of a learning event is a very important practice. They are not setting objectives; they are not designing the course. They are, however, examining the set of objectives provided by the instructors and, in dialogue, telling the instructors and themselves what they hope to learn and achieve in the given time. They name their expectations in pairs or threes. This gives them the opportunity to clarify their own needs for themselves and for their peers. It is a great corroboration when someone else names your expectation before you, and you say, "Yes, that's what I want too!"

These expectations may not be met in the particular learning event. They may, however, become the learning needs assessment for the next course! The instructors can tell participants how they see these expectations might be met in certain learning tasks, and also admit, as necessary, that the training course might not be able to meet those expectations. It is entirely possible to discover that people have come to the wrong course!

The expectations named are used in the formative and summative evaluation of the learning event. At the end of the first day the instructor might ask, "How are we doing so far in relation to your expectations?" At the end of the event, he or she might ask, "How has the course met your expectations?"

Feedback: How to Give It, How to Take It!

Feedback is an important part of adult learning, both as a factor in immediate and long-term evaluation, and as a response to microteaching. As discussed in Task 16 in Chapter Two, adult learners in the training course are invited to examine a set of feedback notes from Training Resources Group (TRG). The notes suggest basically that feedback is best received when it is invited; it is most effective when it is specific rather than general and when it addresses an aspect of the work that people can do something about.

How feedback is given is the issue here. How can the confidence of adult learners be developed, how can they be shown respect, given autonomy by design, and then offered feedback on performance in such a way that the feedback process is congruent with everything else that occurs? The guidelines in the model presented in Chapter Two are very clear about how to give and receive feedback so that it is most helpful. Participants who have designed and led a microteaching session are asked to invite feedback from their peers, and the feedback session is structured according to their wishes. The participants are first invited to do a force field analysis of their team's design and performance, including such questions as, What did you like about your design? About your materials? About your facilitation and teaching process? What would you change next time? This analysis gives them the chance to reflect together on their work, to take the lead in the analysis of it. Then we ask the same questions of those who were the learners: What did you like about the design? About the materials? About the team's facilitation and teaching process? What would you suggest they change next time?

This process, of course, uses the principle of autonomy and all the guidelines suggested by TRG. It is never easy to receive feedback. Adult learners doing Jubilee's courses take them very seriously, and are concerned to learn and improve. They are also sensitive and afraid of "losing face" in a feedback session. Again, memory holds a powerful sway over people. Every instructor can recall a painful feedback session in which someone finally had the chance to "tell someone off." The model presented in this book precludes such an event. The principles of popular education form a staunch wall of safety around the adult learner, so feedback cannot tell them off or put them down.

If learners do not improve their performance, their materials, and their designs in response to feedback, what use is such feedback? In the model presented here, teams immediately design a second microteaching, using and testing the feedback suggestions they have received. This is a very important practice of reinforcement. It is not possible to say what another person wants to do. Feedback that sounds like, "You did not want to listen to the women, so you moved very quickly over that part of the task," is not effective. Although we cannot know what another person wants or wanted to do, we can describe what we saw him do and we can tell how that affected us. "You did not ask any of the women for their ideas. This made me angry. You might be careful to hear from a really diverse sample next time."

All feedback is a consultative vote: the person himself or herself must decide whether he or she can hear the feedback and work with it or not. The appropriate response, therefore, is, "Thank you." When we defend or give reasons or excuses for actions that are being examined through feedback, we create an unreal situation. At the beginning of a feedback session, I suggest that people responding to feedback avoid starting a sentence with "but" and instead start with "Thank you!" and move to the next issue. It is up to the receiver of feedback to do whatever he or she wants with the suggestions offered.

Force Field Analysis: What Works? What Should Be Changed?

A very useful tool for immediate evaluation is *force field analysis*, which comes from the work of Kurt Lewin (1951). Force field analysis invites adult learners to analyze their work in terms of a positive force field and of a negative force field. The instructor sets this up by asking: What was most useful for you in the course today? This question elicits the positive force field that is moving the learners toward their goal, which is implementing the objectives. The instructor then asks, What would you suggest we change? This invites the participants' reflection on what behavior, system, or aspect of the program impeded their progress, and what might be done to overcome the obstacle as the course continues.

Force field analysis is used daily for formative evaluation, and then again at the end of the course for summative evaluation. The participants in one program organized a party to celebrate the completion of the course. At about 11:00 P.M. one of them put up a page of newsprint on the wall of the lounge and asked the dancing, laughing group: "Now what was most useful about this party? And what shall we change next time?"

Found Objects: Whatever Is There Is Useful

Another way to pose the problem that invites adult learners to do critical thinking, analysis, and meaningful learning is to use found objects. While teaching youthful New Yorkers, Ira Shor (1980) wanted to bring a car into the classroom, since it was the epitome of their central theme of adolescent power. He settled on a motorcycle. Adult learners can be invited to use any found objects, anything they can put their hands on, to symbolize their efforts or their family, to show the problems of their community, or to demonstrate their longings for a better life.

Task 1 in Chapter Two presents a simple warm-up that can be used on the first day of a training course. It invites adult learners to select a found object, anything that symbolizes their work in the world. Such an array of manifest creativity and humor and pathos emerges as to frighten a sensitive educator, making him or her realize what a powerful group of adult learners are present. The found objects can stay in place on a central table, reminding the participants of one another's visions of self and work. The objects are revisited at the end of the course, and people are invited to reflect on how their vision has been transformed by the event.

Found objects are especially useful in cross-cultural situations, in which people can show how they are in fact unified in many ways. They are useful when working with preliterate adults, who do not easily use the written word. In Raleigh, North Carolina, the Children's Museum About the World invited a group of youngsters to find objects that represented other nations. They were quite ingenious in what they presented: articles of clothing made in Taiwan, crafts from Latin America and Africa, chocolates from England! The children were quickly made aware, by the easy selection of found objects, how directly related they were to other nations of the world.

Gallery Walk: Revisit, Review

A gallery walk is a review of charts, documents, and pictures posted on the walls. Participants are invited to walk in pairs around the room and to accomplish a learning task in dialogue. The gallery walk is an efficient means to welcome newcomers who arrive after the opening session.

Generative Themes: They're Playing Our Song

As discussed in Task 7 in Chapter Two and elsewhere, generative themes are those ideas and issues, problems and joys that people talk about, worry about, and celebrate. Generative themes are found in the learning needs assessment, in the first task where learners use found objects to describe their work in the world, in the chats at lunch, and in the coffee breaks. Paulo Freire (1993) makes the point that such themes are rooted in the reality of the learners, in their daily world. Instructors in popular education cannot neglect such themes with impunity. These themes are the basis of dialogue.

Group Task Maintenance: A Group Moves on Two Wheels

As participants work in small groups, it is imperative to examine what is going on in these groups. Jubilee uses a simple conceptual framework, the bicycle, whose two wheels represent two vital aspects of each group: task maintenance, or getting the job done, and group maintenance, protecting and nurturing the group that is doing the job.

Each small group is instructed to be somewhat self-conscious for a while as they work, noticing who is doing what toward both task and group maintenance. When this is done early on in a learning process, adult learners can be more explicit about their immediate feelings and needs. There is no need for intense navel gazing, but there is constant need for awareness about the group process. This simple framework offers more than enough for people to hold onto throughout the training course.

Humility: Only the Student Can Name the Moment of the Death of the Professor

This principle was suggested by graduate students in the School of Public Health at UNC, Chapel Hill. They said that the examination of all of these principles and practices made them realize that they would have to give up their power as "professors" in the health clinics and refugee camps and senior centers where they worked. They would not be in charge, but in service to the adult learners they hoped to teach. They accused me, rightfully, of demanding from them an attitude of humility that was somewhat incongruent with their prestige as masters of public health. I reminded them of all the times during the term they had told me to be quiet or to wait while they completed their small group work around a complex learning task. I reminded them of the very difficult three-hour class when they twice called me in as a resource to their small-group work for a five-minute consultation!

Humility, the sages tell us, is truth. The truth is, it is not easy for anyone to give up the mantle of power as the "professor." The truth also is that without the moment of realization that comes to adults, that they must apply new knowledge, skills, and attitudes for themselves in their own way, there is no critical learning.

I agree with these graduate students, that humility is a vital principle in this approach to adult learning. There is no course entitled Humility 401, but you will inevitably learn it as you begin to examine and apply this model to your own adult education events.

Humor: No Laughing, No Learning

In El Salvador the wise planners of a training course had a line item in their budget for hiring a band for dancing. That kind of wisdom is rare. Something that is also needed in the budget is humor. As adults learn, as they open the vistas of their value systems and cognitive frames and affective potential to an unknown, they need humor to get them across the borders.

Humor not only lightens, it enlightens. As adult learners struggle with new concepts, skills, and attitudes, they need to laugh at themselves in their "new clothes," or at the large number of emperors walking around in the buff. When we can chuckle at our own pompous statements of certainty and laugh at our ridiculous application of theory to practice, we can relax enough to identify and examine what is in fact uncertain, and to test novel applications of theory to practice.

The best parts of each training course are those memorable moments of incongruity when the trainer or one of the participants did something to bring the house down. None of the profoundly serious moments is ever remembered so well.

A team of women doing a microteaching at a recent course discovered themselves almost literally drowning in newsprint. They had charts of their charts! Newsprint was peeling from the walls and dropping into the middle of the floor. It was impossible for them to discover which chart was first and which was thirty-first. Finally, they threw up their hands in despair and laughed until they cried. They will never use too much newsprint again, nor will any of the other adult learners who shared their laughing and learning.

The celebration of such events with humor demands ego strength. I very intentionally tell the learners about my own errors and escapades in the preparation of the course: how I left a videotape I was to use on the kitchen table, how I took a wrong turn and nearly missed the exit, how I continually mixed up the names of two young men in a group. Such expressions of humanness and humor help adult learners to realize that their errors will be treated with equal ease. If we cannot laugh at ourselves, we cannot really do this work of helping adults learn.

Immediacy: How Soon Can We Use This?

With achievement-based objectives, learners use the new content immediately, within the training session, and know that they know it because they have in fact used it. Such immediacy makes for high motivation. I have often heard participants in training courses say, "This is not only for my work. This is for my life." Immediacy! Without immediacy there is a dullness in the learning situation. The participants are there, but not there. They put in time and take the examinations or do what is needed to "pass" the course, but there is no verve, no excitement about what they are learning.

All decisions about content, methods, learning tasks, and materials are directed by this principle of immediacy. If a skill or attitude is not immediately useful to an adult, it is probably not being learned as effectively as possible. How can immediacy be built in?

In the example of the Chilean medical school program presented in Chapter Three, the health professionals who were the participants were invited to design the training for village health aides they would do as soon as they returned to their field stations and clinics. The learning task within the training was immediate, for application tomorrow! Immediacy was transformed in this instance from an abstract principle to an operative decision-forming device.

Inductive/Deductive Learning: Where Do We Begin?

A deductive approach begins with theory and invites practice to prove the hypothesis that is the theory. An inductive approach begins with practice and evokes the theory as a hypothesis to explain the rationale in the practice. Which approach is better? Is an inductive or a deductive approach used in participatory, accountable adult learning? The answer is "Yes!" Both are used interchangeably, constantly, and intentionally in this popular education model. Intentionally is the operative word. It is the task of educators to decide which of the two approaches will be used, and to be prepared to give a sound reason for the choice.

In the popular education model presented in Chapter Two and in the diverse examples provided in Chapters Three through Nine there is constant movement between the inductive and the deductive approaches. Some learning tasks begin with the theory and show examples and applications of it (deductive), and some begin with examples and do an analysis that evokes either known theory or new theory. I think of the process as more a circulation than a single linear movement. One approach invites the other as a consequence.

When teachers/trainers defend their choice of where to begin, using such language as, "I set out the problem so that they could analyze it and see the need through this inductive approach for the theory I aim to teach," they are indicating that they comprehend the differences and can use both approaches.

Inclusion: Is Everyone on Board?

It is the responsibility of the instructor to assure inclusion by the design of the training. There is only one alternative to inclusion: exclusion. When an adult learner feels excluded, little or no learning takes place. This principle is clearly related to respect, immediacy, relevance, and accountability. All of these principles are kissing cousins!

A remarkable incident occurred in Tanzania during a training of church leaders. Small groups of men and women had been formed to do a learning task. I watched as they set out to work. In one group an elderly woman, well dressed in typical Tanzanian garb, was slowly moving her chair out of her group. It was such a gradual movement that no one in the group noticed it. I went over and asked the entire group: "What is happening here?" "Where? What?" they all asked. Maria, the elderly woman, stopped her unconscious motion, but her chair was by now six feet from her group. Her colleagues were surprised. "Where are you going, Maria? What's the matter?" When we talked the situation through we discovered that the group had decided to use Swahili in their discussions, and Maria, who spoke the local language, Kihaya, did not speak Swahili. She felt excluded and was unconsciously manifesting her feelings in her quiet locomotion out of the group. They quickly resolved the difficulty by switching to Kihaya, the common language of everyone in the group, and Maria joined in with gusto.

Feelings of exclusion are not often so manifest. How can instructors assure that the principle of inclusion is at work in their courses so that such feelings do not arise? Small groups can be used and norms about language and participation can be established. Care can be taken to affirm each person's contribution and call each by name. Each gesture of respect and courtesy is an expression of inclusion. A major problem in adult education in many countries around the world is the disappearance of learners after a few weeks in a course. They come with great expectations, find that they are not intentionally, personally included, and ultimately exclude themselves from the program. Statistics on dropouts from adult learning events are appalling. The principle and practice of inclusion could help here.

Learning Tasks: We Learn by Doing

This is an axiom of adult learning: adults learn by doing. The learning task is a way to learn concepts, by presenting material through handouts, charts, illustrated lectures, stories, maps, overhead projections of graphs or handouts, and video or audio presentations, and then inviting the adult learners to do something with the information, immediately. For example, adult learners can be taught about revised tax laws by using a handout and an overhead projection to present the facts, with a set of questions: What are your questions? Describe how this will affect your tax payments this year. How would you explain this change to your son by using an example of the change in payments?

While learning tasks are often done in small task groups, the sharing of the results is done in the large group, with comments from the instructor. It is useful to use a sample when sharing the results of small group work. A sample means that a few of the groups share their responses.

It is important to repeat that the learning task is a task for the learners. I see too many designs prepared by teachers and trainers in which the tasks describe what the teacher is going to do.

Needs Assessment: Who Needs What as Defined by Whom?

The needs assessment is both a principle and a practice. The principle is vital to an effective adult learning event. The practice is done using diverse modes: telephone surveys, videotaped focus groups, audiotaped interviews, and written surveys. In teaching the principle, Jubilee uses a simple triangle as a model, inviting learners to consider three aspects of learning needs assessment: ask, study, and observe.

Hearing the personal perception of the training session from a sample of learners often surprises the instructor. As illustrated in both the generic model and in the various case studies in this book, Jubilee does such a needs assessment prior to the beginning of a training course. If possible, we also visit the work site or the community to observe the participants in action. We study all the documentation we can find on the group or the organization. We then do a learning task on day one, inviting participants to share their expectations in light of the set achievement-based objectives and the program plan. Their expression of their expectations will not immediately change the plan, but these expectations will be taken into consideration as the course proceeds.

The importance of the needs assessment is linked to all the other principles: the learner as subject, dialogue, problem-posing, relevance. It has an immense subjective value in that the adult learners immediately feel listened to and vital, which they are. Once, while doing a needs assessment telephone survey prior to a strategic planning workshop for a large hospital, Jubilee discovered that the burning issue among the professional staff was the fear of an upcoming merger that might cut out their jobs. Jubilee had had no word of that possible merger from the administrator who had invited us to do the course at that time. We were able to talk with the hospital director and put off the course until the decision on the merger had been made. Thus, the needs assessment activity had provided vitally important information about the entire enterprise. This example also shows how important it is to take a diverse sample from among the participants, to get different perspectives. Administrators will have a different view of a situation than the nurses, who will differ in their perspective from the social workers. Celebrate this diversity, and use it in selecting a sample for the needs assessment.

Open Questions: Invite Dialogue

The open question is a most effective means of inviting dialogue. An open question is one that does not have a predetermined response. An open question invites critical reflection, analysis, review, and personal perceptions. A closed question, conversely, invites the "correct" answer. Closed questions stop dialogue, invite monologue, and put the authority of knowing back onto the teacher.

Learning tasks for adult learners are open questions accompanied by the resources they need to respond. In a seminar with lawyers in Zimbabwe, I showed them a large wall map of the city of Harare and its surroundings. The map had demographic information and showed industrial and agricultural enclaves. The learning task was to work in small task groups of three people each, to decide what three parts of the urban capital had the greatest need for lawyers' services, and to tell why they have named those parts. As the participants responded to these open questions, they learned a great deal about their city and the needs of major populations. They used the printed resources about the city and their own experience, knowledge, and values to develop a new attitude and new knowledge about their environment. The intense engagement within the learning groups and their passionate sharing of their decisions manifested how well the open questions had worked and how much the participants knew they knew.

There is a place for closed questions. Teachers must simply be aware of what they do to the learner and to the teacher. There is a place for open questions as well, and teachers must also be aware of what *they* do to the learner and to the teacher. The task is to know which to use at what time.

Since open questions invite dialogue, and a learning task is an open question, this approach to adult learning uses open questions lavishly. The model presented in Chapter Two demonstrates how to use open questions effectively in adult education and training.

Praxis: How Does Praxis Make Perfect?

Praxis means action with reflection. It combines the inductive and deductive approaches to learning. Praxis invites an examination of an action just completed so that relevant theory can be applied. The cycle of praxis is (1) do; (2) look at what you did; (3) reflect using theory; (4) change; (5) do, and so on. Praxis is not practice, which could be a repetition of a given approach without the reflective analysis and new dimensions.

Here is an example of praxis: In a training course, one purpose is to develop the skill of designing and producing clear, effective visual aids. Using a gallery walk, pairs of participants are invited to examine all of the visuals on the walls and to grade them for clarity and effectiveness. Each pair then shares their grades with the others, and the entire group devises a checklist of ways to assure clear and effective visuals. Finally, each pair makes a visual using the ways determined.

The model presented in Chapter Two includes a learning task that invites participants to design a learning event, make teaching/ learning materials, and teach the group. This microteaching is teaching praxis, not practice teaching, because the most useful moment is the reflection on the design and teaching. The feedback session is set up with questions that stimulate praxis: What did you do ? What did you see happening as a result of it? What did you like? What would you change in the light of the principles and practices you have been learning? When every learning task is a praxis, you will have immediacy and relevance and highly motivated learning. This activity is another example of how the training course has to model the principles and practices in order to teach them.

Preparation: Two to One!

The hardest part of accountable adult education is the preparation. As noted in Chapter Two and elsewhere, preparation for a course takes twice as much time as the course itself. That is, it takes ten days to prepare a five-day training program. Unless educators are willing to put that kind of time into the design and preparation of an event, they cannot use this popular education approach to accountable adult learning.

How is the time spent? At Jubilee, we begin the process by creating a basic program from our experience. This we send to our clients. They review it, asking questions, adding new items as they see fit, thus changing and reshaping the program. We take their input and refine the program further. This plan goes out to all participants, whom we then interview by telephone, inviting their reflections on the achievement-based objectives and the program plan. We have been studying the composition of the group, their work experience and education profiles, so we know to whom we are speaking. Adult learners always remark that this telephone survey of their personal impressions of the program and their expectations is very important to them. They feel honored and respected at the start. The dialogue has begun!

Fueled by their responses, we go back to the program and make further changes. Then we start doing the research needed and making the learning materials: stories, critical incidents, case studies, pictures, handouts of content, and charts of all the learning tasks. We make place cards for each participant, which will be used to set up the initial table teams. The workshop materials are set out in a course book for each individual student, in the sequence in which the materials will be used.

When two instructors are working together, it is imperative that each know just what his or her role is: who will lead which learning task, who will do what work with small groups, with flip charts, with video or audio. The preparation of roles and tasks can avoid a great deal of confusion that can hurt the learning potential.

Preparation also involves visiting the site of the session, checking on heating and cooling, tables and chairs, materials, controls of room temperature, and food preparation and procurement if necessary. It means knowing who the contact person is at the site in case there is a problem or an accident. Preparation involves setting up and documenting a library of resources that adult learners can use during the course, and determining who will be responsible for tracking borrowed books. If certain training sessions are repeated, it is wise to establish protocols for such procedures.

Preparation also means taking time out before a major training event to relax and clear your mind of details so you can see the forest for the trees. The quality of preparation will be evident as soon as adult learners enter the room for the educational event.

Relevance: Who Needs What as Defined by Whom?

In Knowles's (1980) research, relevance was the second most important factor in adult learning. Adults will learn faster and more permanently that which is significant to them and to their present lives. The trainer's task often is not to change what we wish to teach but to make it relevant by connecting the content to the themes and knowledge of the learners.

Selection of participants for any training session is done with attention to relevance. The operative question is, how is this new knowledge, how are these new skills and attitudes, relevant to the learning needs of these adults? How do they see them as relevant? Teachers may see significant relevance of particular content to a group of adults, but if the adults themselves do not see that relevance, it does not exist. Again, part of the instructor's job is to demonstrate that relevance by making connections to learners' themes.

In North Carolina, working with a troubled nonprofit group, I set out a standard set of activities on communication skills. The participants had said that this was what they wanted and needed. However, it soon became apparent that this set of skills was not relevant to the learners, who felt safe in communicating with one another but were enraged at the failure of the top management of the nonprofit to communicate with staff. The only relevant learning for them at the moment had to do with organizational development, not communications.

Relevance is directly related to immediacy, the third of Knowles's factors in adult learning. If adults do not see the relevance of content, no matter how crucial that content is to the teacher, the learners quickly determine that they do not need to know it.

The principles and practices of popular education obviously work together to form a coherent whole and a process that has its own character. The principle of relevance is one vital part of that process. A learning needs assessment is not merely a time to discover the skills and knowledge level of participants and their learning needs. It is also a time to discover their generative themes, their issues, their culture, their language, and their world, so that whatever is taught fits somehow into that world. The paradox is that teachers cannot lead people out of their own boundaries until they present the wider world to the learners in terms of those boundaries.

I think with some shame and contrition of my own years teaching mathematics to high school girls in rural Tanzania using the classic green textbook by Parr published and produced in the United Kingdom. The examples went something like this: If the train in the underground moves at twenty-four miles per hour. . . . It is crucial not to repeat that kind of insolent irrelevance in designing for educating adults today.

Accountability insists on preparation that creates a context for a group of adult learners in which the instructors can show how the knowledge, skills, and attitudes they are teaching fit into the participants' lives. Nothing is so strong a motivator for adult learning as this manifest relevance. Freire puts it this way: "It is to the reality which mediates men [sic], and to the perception of that reality held by educators and people, that we must go to find the program content of education" (1993, p. 77).

Respect: How Do You Spell Respect?

Knowles's (1980) early research shows that respect is the prime factor in adult learning. If learners do not feel respected by the teacher, they will not learn what they might learn. How is respect shown to adult learners? How is this prime factor modeled in a training course? Jubilee begins the process of showing respect in our telephone or fax survey of prospective students by inviting their response to the program they have seen, their sense of their own needs, and their awareness of their strengths. We prepare place cards for all participants, and have materials marked with their names. We welcome everyone as they enter, having arranged a time for people to meet informally around some pleasant food. We correspond at length with participants before they come to the program, to make sure that it is what they really need and want.

Another word for respect is courtesy. Respect is a principle that, like all others, transcends culture. Visitors to Ethiopia do not show respect in the same way as do visitors in Chile, but they do show respect. The task of the educator is to discover how to show "respect" in a particular culture.

Once, in a training course in Ethiopia, the young men who were the participants were reluctant to use the participative popular education approach in the villages because, as they explained, "The women will not talk to us men." I urged them to do all they could to show respect, and to be prepared for the surprise when the women did take part and tell their perspectives. The young trainees went out, two by two, to villages in the hills to do their first session. I accompanied one pair of youthful community educators. Men and women leaders of the village took part in the session and were invited to respond to open questions. As the men had anticipated, the women did not talk for a long while. Then we heard a very small, low-pitched voice from the corner. When the leader turned to the woman who had spoken, she waved him away. The other young man moved gently toward the speaker and sat on a low bench near her. Another provocative question, another weak sound from the same veiled woman. The instructor, with infinite gentleness and respect, indicated that he had not heard what she said. The woman looked around the group, and glanced appreciatively at the young man at her side before she spoke with a loud, clear voice. For the rest of that community meeting, men and women spoke with equal strength. I could not understand the Amharic dialogue, but I knew that those quiet signs of respect from the young men in a mountain village in northern Ethiopia had worked.

What are the indicators that adults feel respected in a learning event? Obviously, they speak up. Then they grow fearless. They talk out of turn and ask tough questions. They dispute the position of the instructor and they make unexpected applications of the content. They suggest changes in the program to align it more closely to their needs. They speak their heart. As you can see, respect is a dangerous as well as a powerful factor in adult learning. The six diverse examples in Part Two demonstrate how remarkably this respect works. Trainers often complain that the systems they work in are themselves disrespectful. A training session cannot set out to change systems. Systems can, however, be transformed by creating new systems based on respect. Popular education is political action, and there is no place where such a transformation of the power base is seen in a training course as when adult learners, feeling respected and sensing their own power, take over. For the educator, this is an exciting as well as uncomfortable time. We have not yet tested the hypothesis that such mutual respect can transform oppressive systems. We know that without mutual respect revolutions have failed.

Reinforcement: 1,142 Times!

Reinforcement is another basic and vital principle for adult learning. The learner needs not only time for mastering new knowledge, skills, and attitudes, but she or he also needs to have this mastery reinforced at every possible opportunity. How long does it take to know something well? How many times must one repeat a skill or a set of concepts and facts or a new attitude before it is one's own? The job of the educator is to design that reinforcement task. Jubilee has a saying: do it 1,142 times and you have got it! Every learning design must have lots of intentional reinforcement tasks for the learners. Learning is an iterative process.

In a graduate course at the School of Public Health at UNC, Chapel Hill, I teach young adults the seven steps of planning as a tool for organizing a learning session. Invariably, it is during their individual community project, as they design a learning session in health for community adults, that they say: "Oh, I see, the learning task is a task for the learner!"

Carl Jung teaches that the psyche knows no time (Jung, 1969). The attitudes, habits, and conceptions we learned or formed long ago are still at work and need intense, conscious effort to transform them. That intense effort is shored up by reinforcement and by the iterative nature of this process.

Role Plays/Sociodrama: The Play's the Thing!

There is nothing so powerful as a well-designed sociodrama (a drama based on a social issue) or a role play (an improvised drama in which participants take specific roles—you are the mother, you are the teenage son who wants to drive the new car); there is also nothing quite so dangerous. Role plays are used with great caution in the model and the examples presented in this book. The reason for that is the simple fact that no human being can simulate a feeling. Feelings are always real. Role plays and sociodramas evoke strong feelings. These feelings must be dealt with. Teachers often find themselves in therapeutic situations in which everyone moves through a catharsis and comes out on the other side stronger and more in touch with themselves. Educators of adults are not therapists, however. Few are trained in that specialized discipline that enables the therapist not only to evoke but also to analyze and channel strong feelings.

In my long experience in adult education, I have seen too many teachers get into corners from which they could not make a graceful exit for themselves or for their adult learners. I therefore teach adult educators to use sociodrama and role play in conjunction with very intentional use of all the other principles and practices. Consider where such a sociodrama might lead. Feel the feelings such role plays might evoke. Consider how you will deal with these feelings. I suggest that it is better to give up a powerful learning experience than put vulnerable adults into risks they cannot overcome. It is like inviting volunteer firemen to practice in a real burning building. You cannot put them too close to the fire, no matter how useful a learning experience it might be.

Safety: Safety First!

There is an interesting contradiction between the risk involved in learning faced by any adult and their need for safety. Jung (1969) challenges us to hold the opposites. People need both challenge and safety. When the learning environment does not appear safe to adult learners, they will disappear, or resist the program dramatically to protect themselves. The effort to provide a safe environment involves respect, calling adults by name, asking their expectations of a learning program, asking for regular feedback on the process, affirming their contributions. Experience has shown that the absence of safety is a factor in declining attendance, and that the presence of safety is a factor in enhanced learning.

Sequence: Who's on First?

Sequence is a vital principle in designing educational events. Jubilee suggests the following sequences: simple to more complex, easy to more difficult, slowly to more quickly, A to B. Nothing is more confusing for an adult learner than a design that is out of sequence. There are some unyielding conditions for learning and this is one of them: you can get there from here if you take ordered steps.

Many people remember a computer course in which the instructor assumed we knew the macro keys and continually invited us to use F4 without explanation until a brave soul pointed out that his lesson was out of sequence. Until the instructor went back and solved for us the mystery of macro keys, we were not going to learn anything that day. The instructor was putting the proverbial cart before the horse.

Using sequence means reflecting hard on a design to see that the learning tasks mesh well together: first the learners do this, then this, then this. Without the principle of sequence, one cannot judge the order of learning tasks. Every design needs to be tested through the web of all the principles, but especially through the fine-mesh web of sequence. When adult learners look at you with question marks on their faces and confusion in their eyes, you can be sure you need to reexamine your sequence.

Silence: Have You Ever Tried Silence?

This question was put to me by Trish Swift, a Quaker friend in Zimbabwe, after an energetic and lively training session with a group of law professors from the University of Zimbabwe Law School. Trish had come to observe, and in her feedback she shared her concern that the pace and energy had left little time for reflection on the new theories being explored.

Silence offers both learners and teachers the occasion for that exploration. It can be achieved in a number of ways. For example, before an evaluation task, participants can be invited to go outside and walk in the woods or around the streets for a few moments, listening to their own hearts, their own thoughts, their own feelings about both what was learned and how it was being taught and learned. After an open question is asked, the group may be invited to hold their responses for five minutes, to reflect on the significance of the question and of their forthcoming answers. After a warmup—for example, after people name the symbols of their work—take five minutes to quietly reflect on all of them in silence. Then ask the question: What strikes you about all these symbols?

Silence offers opportunity for quiet reflection on new concepts, the implications of newly tried skills, and the challenge of new attitudes. As a fourth century saint (Augustine of Hippo) once put it: no one teaches another man anything. All we do is prepare the way for the work of the Spirit. That work is often done in silence.

During a graduate course in adult education for health professionals, I once sat quietly with the group after a particularly painful and insightful comment by one of them about the distance they felt between them and their minority, poverty-stricken clients. We sat in silence that was not awkward, but rather profound and stimulating at the same time. Wheels were turning! Men and women were permitting their imaginations and memories to run back and to run forward. A young man with three years of Peace Corps experience in West Africa finally said: "Let me tell a story." The group sighed a corporate sigh and said, "Please do!" Our silence had been fruitful. It often is.

Skills, Knowledge, Attitudes

These are the content of a course. They are often represented by a series of nouns or verbal nouns, for example, how to give and take feedback; the uses of silence; echoing; the design of learning tasks; and respect. These are some of the knowledge sets, the skills and the attitudes taught in the training workshop. Sometimes they are called KAP: knowledge, attitudes, and psychomotor skills.

Content is designed and articulated in response to the question, "What are you teaching?" Here is where the research is done, where the empirical base of what is being taught is confirmed. When the content is clearly set out, the achievement-based objectives are simply what the learners will do with that content in order to learn it; for example, participants will have practiced echoing, or will have named ways to show respect to others in the small groups.

Small Groups: A Place of Safety for Learning and Sharing

The small group is indeed a place of safety. Instructors cannot know who among the adult participants is an introvert, who an extrovert. In spite of all the effort put into a learning needs assessment, the background and experience of all participants cannot be fully known. Most adult human beings can deal with two or three other adults; most adult human beings fall silent in a group of twelve or more.

This model of popular education and all of the examples in this book show the use of small learning groups. People do learning tasks with one another, working as a team. They therefore learn from one another. The locus of power in such a physical situation shifts from the podium to the small group. Watch this happen as you use this popular education approach. There is physical safety in the small group. People often say more and learn more in the small group than they could possibly share in the larger class. The small group is a place to practice freedom, autonomy, cooperation, and mutual acceptance.

The small group tasks raise energy very visibly. If the instructor offers a lengthy explanation and invites people to simply turn to one another (in pairs) and name their questions, a physical and spiritual change takes place in the energy in the room. People are engaged, they become animated and critical, practicing autonomy as they name their own idiosyncratic questions, and listening to their colleagues.

I think back to the brilliant lectures on William Blake that Professor Marius Bewley offered at Fordham University in the early sixties to a large graduate class of adult students. I imagine the transformation of that room had he known the potential of the small group task to get adults actively engaged in a critique and an application of his powerful insights. The learning task in the small group is the instructor's way of inviting adult learners to do something with that ripe moment, together!

How are such groups set up? They can be arranged arbitrarily, simply pulling names from a hat and putting four people at a table. They can be arranged using some homogeneous criteria: by gender, putting all the men together and all the women together; by age, putting all the seniors together and all the younger folks together; or by job, putting all the accountants together and all the social workers together. The learners themselves can be invited to find three other people with whom to sit. There are numerous ways to organize small groups. The important thing is to organize them intentionally, in a manner appropriate to the group and the purpose of the event.

For some learning tasks, the small group may have a recorder. Ideally, this role can shift from one person to another as needed.

When small groups are doing a meaningful learning task, there will be a healthy sense of competition among them. This is a healthy, normal, constructive element in adult learning. Destructive competition means you lose, I win. As we work to affirm and celebrate the efforts of adult learners, all groups know that they know; all win.

Small task groups were invited to present a mime to summarize a reading they had just done in a workshop on leadership. This activity led to a fascinating sense of competition: each mime presented was more creative and charming than the last. They learned from one another at an alarming and manifest pace.

The small task group is a place to risk, to dare, to complain, to argue, to clarify, and to question. There are ways to do group maintenance, inviting adult learners to be conscious of who talks and who does not, who initiates and who follows, who seems to be left out, who provides the humor and laughter, and who gets them to move to action. Task maintenance in the small group involves someone taking responsibility to begin the task, to clarify it, to move it to completion and evaluation. As groups mature, this group/task maintenance is a natural phenomenon. At the outset of an event with this kind of learning, it is wise to review these "rules of the road."

How often should the composition of small groups be changed? I like to leave that to the adult learners to decide. They have the best sense of their own safety needs and of their own capacity for meeting and working with new people. Remember one axiom: when a new person enters a group, there is a new group.

Snow Cards: Small Notes on Wall

This is a useful technique. Learners put one item on a single white card and post it. This invites their physical effort, their choice as subjects, and offers the prospect of clustering the gathered cards as needed. Someone suggested that snow cards were so named because the cards were white; another said it means "small notes on wall." In any case, they are a useful and inexpensive practice for brainstorming or reporting of any kind.

Subject: Never an Object

Paulo Freire bases his problem-posing approach to adult learning on the assumption that human beings are subjects or decision makers in their own lives. The opposite of being a subject in one's own life is feeling like an object, a thing used by others. This is to me the central concept of popular education: adults are decision makers in their own lives, and every part of educational design is to invite them to make decisions, to practice being the subjects they are. This concept explains why all education is political.

Synthesis: Putting It All Together

This is both a principle and a practice. At some time it is necessary to set a learning task that puts it all together, that synthesizes what has been learned. This could be called a recapitulation, or a summary task. It makes sense to use the word synthesis, since throughout the training course, analysis is used as a way to take concepts, skills, and attitudes apart in order to learn them. For example, when teaching the seven steps of planning and ways to design a problem-posing, dialogical approach to teaching adults, participants can be invited to do a design, to actually use what they have learned in a synthesis activity. Most adult learners say that this is where the learning really takes place for them, in the synthesis task.

Participants are invited to learn piece by piece in all the learning tasks, then they are invited to put it all together and do something with what they have learned in a synthesis task. This task is a very important piece of the puzzle; it is not, however, a test. It is a way for participants to prove to themselves that they know they know.

In the Himalayan mountains of Nepal, I was doing a long training course for community development workers. On the final day of the course, they were celebrating all they had learned when I told them we had one more learning task: they were to work in pairs, using the seven steps of planning, to design a two-hour workshop for their colleagues in the office in Katmandu, teaching them one skill they themselves had learned in the course. They groaned with delight, sorry at having to get to work on this last day, delighted to show how skilled they had become in designing accountable learning. They did it in an amazingly short time, and knew that they knew!

Time: You Old Beggar Man

Is this one, perhaps, the most important principle? I think so. As I stated earlier, I like to advise teachers that there are three vital principles for accountable adult learning, in this order: time, time, and time. Even while we honor the fact that all learning is idiosyncratic, and offer respect and build in immediacy and relevance, we need to give adult learners time to learn what we are teaching them. The pace of an adult learning session will indicate how aware the teacher is of this principle: is it hurried, harried, moving rapidly toward the teacher's 'covering' all that he or she wanted to teach? Or is it reflective, quiet, respectful of the questions and concerns of the learners? Just as learning is idiosyncratic, so indeed is teaching.

Each educator has his or her own personality and natural pace. The principle of time, however, invites teachers to accommodate their natural, personal style to the needs of adult learners. In a recent graduate course, which is in fact a train-the-trainers program, the group took decisive action in inviting me to drop a large segment of the program so that they might more thoroughly do another segment which they felt was being neglected for lack of time. In this case, they had the deliberative vote: they made the decision. I had a consultative vote, offering the suggestion that they read the materials presented for the segment they elected to omit. The individual adult must decide what is possible for him or her in the time given. The task of teachers and designers of participative, accountable adult education is to keep the system open enough for learners to review, analyze, and decide. The responsibility to learn is theirs. The responsibility of the educators is to listen, to urge, to support, and to celebrate, all of which takes time.

In all of the microteaching I have seen people do in training courses, the greatest problem they have faced is what they called "lack of time." Adults constantly try to teach more than people can learn, to attempt more than people can do, to set out more work than can be accomplished in a given amount of time. "If I only had enough time" is not a reason for not achieving an educational objective. It can be an excuse. At Jubilee, when we review designs, we often point out that we see too much content for the time frame, that is, too much "what" for the "when." In the seven steps of planning, the question "when" is the operative question, controlling the designer's response to "what for" (the objectives) and "what" (the content). The time factor is taken into consideration when making achievement-based objectives to teach content accountably.

Title: What's in a Name?

Any learning event, workshop, course, or seminar needs to have a title that will clearly indicate what the event is all about. The title is a fine marketing device, drawing adults into the session. In the same way, it avoids having people come to a session only to discover it is not what they had expected.

Titles must be clear and unambiguous, compelling and challenging. Adults want to know that they will learn something worthwhile in exchange for their time and effort. Jubilee offers an effective, short workshop to industry and nonprofit groups called "We've Got to Stop Meeting Like This: Guidelines for Effective Meetings." Humor in a title is useful, but it must not obscure the heart of the matter.

Each chart you use in a training event must also have a title, for example, "Task 4: How Adults Learn." If you forget to give a title to a chart, the learners may find the material ambiguous and confusing.

Warm-Up: Let's Get Started Safely and Slowly

The warm-up to an adult learning session is the first learning task, to focus adult learners on the topic, to divest them of preoccupations and distractions, to move them into the learning action.

The warm-up is a learning task. Some warm-up questions include: What made you come to this program? What found object symbolizes your work in this world? Who would you like to have taking this course with you? What do you hope to do with these new skills when you finish here? Which of these different-colored cloths would you select to symbolize adult learning for you?

The warm-up is a subjective task, inviting people to identify and share what they wish of their own mood and feeling toward the learning process. It is a good means for clarifying their purposes and for honoring them.

It is important that the warm-up task be congruent with the issue at hand. If the group is studying new tax forms, the warm-up has to do with taxes. If the session is a training program to learn how to teach adults, the warm-up is about the participants' lives and work and their own learning. Warm-up tasks are usually short. Our axiom suggests: a warm-up is a learning task and it is based on the topic of the course.

References

Beamish, J., and Vella, J. *Developing Health Journalists*. Research Triangle Park, N.C.: Family Health International, 1993.

Brookfield, S. *Adult Learners, Adult Education, and the Community*. New York: Columbia University Teachers College, 1984.

Brookfield, S. *Understanding and Facilitating Adult Learning: A Comprehensive Analysis of Principles and Effective Practices*. San Francisco: Jossey-Bass, 1986.

Brookfield, S. *Developing Critical Thinkers: Challenging Adults to Explore New Ways of Thinking and Acting*. San Francisco: Jossey-Bass, 1987.

Brookfield S. *The Skillful Teacher: On Technique, Trust, and Responsiveness in the Classroom*. San Francisco: Jossey-Bass, 1990.

Campbell, J., and Moyers, B. *The Power of Myth*. New York: Doubleday, 1988.

Freire, P. *Cultural Action for Freedom*. Cambridge, Mass.: Harvard Educational Review, Monograph Series No. 1, 1970.

Freire, P. *Education as the Practice of Freedom*. London: Writers and Readers, 1976.

Freire, P. *Pedagogy of the Oppressed, Twentieth Anniversary Edition*. New York: Continuum, 1993. (Orig. New York: Seabury, 1972.)

Freire, P., and Shor, I. *A Pedagogy for Liberation: Dialogues on Transforming Education*. New York: Bergin and Garvey, 1987.

James, M., and Jongeward, D. *Born to Win*. Reading, Mass.: Addison-Wesley, 1975.

Johnson, D., and Johnson, F. *Joining Together: Group Theory and Group Skills*. rev. ed. Englewood Cliffs, N.J.: Prentice Hall, 1991.

Jung, C. *The Collected Works*. Princeton, N.J.: Princeton University Press, 1969.

Knowles, M. *Self-Directed Learning: A Guide for Learners and Teachers*. Chicago: Follett, 1975.

Knowles, M. *The Adult Learner: A Neglected Species*. Houston, Tex.: Gulf, 1978.

Knowles, M. *The Modern Practice of Adult Education*. rev. ed. New York: Cambridge Book Co., 1980.

Knowles, M. *The Making of an Adult Educator: An Autobiographical Journey*. San Francisco: Jossey-Bass, 1989.

Knox, A. *Developing, Administering, and Evaluating Adult Education*. San Francisco: Jossey-Bass, 1980.

Knox, A. *Helping Adults Learn: A Guide to Planning, Implementing, and Conducting Programs*. San Francisco: Jossey-Bass, 1986.

Lewin, K. *Field Theory in Social Science*. New York: HarperCollins, 1951.

Maslow, A. *Motivation and Personality*. New York: HarperCollins, 1954.

Miller, A. *Death of a Salesman*. New York: Viking, 1949.

Moore, T. *Care of the Soul*. New York: HarperCollins, 1992.

Oliver, D. *Education and Community*. Berkeley, Calif.: McCutchan, 1976.

Oliver, D., with Gershman, K. W. *Education, Modernity, and Fractured Meaning*. Albany, N.Y.: SUNY Press, 1989.

Price, R. *A Whole New Life*. New York: Atheneum, 1994.

Schön, D. *The Reflective Practitioner: How Professionals Think in Action*. New York: Basic Books, 1982.

Shor, I. *Critical Teaching and Everyday Life*. Boston: South End Pr., 1980.

Srinivasan, L. *Options for Educators: A Monograph for Decision Makers on Alternative Participative Strategies*. New York: PACT, 1992.

Vella, J. *Learning to Listen*. Amherst: Center for International Development, University of Massachusetts, 1979.

Vella, J. *Learning to Teach*. Westport, Conn.: Save the Children, 1989.

Vella, J. *Learning to Listen to Mothers*. Washington, D.C.: Academy for Educational Development, 1992.

Vella, J. *Learning to Listen, Learning to Teach: The Power of Dialogue in Educating Adults*. San Francisco: Jossey-Bass, 1994.

Webster's Tenth New Collegiate Dictionary. Springfield, Mass.: Merriam Webster, 1994.

Index

U

U.S. AID, 81

V

Vella, J., 17, 48, 60, 62, 64, 86, 109, 112,
   113, 114, 125, 146
Vindasius, J., 107, 108
Visual aids, 157–158
Voice, consultative/deliberative, 7, 37, 67
Vote, consultative/deliberative, 160

W

Walker, R., 59, 69, 70
Warm-up, 195–196; in popular education
   training model, 16–17, 37, 45; in
   training programs, 62, 66, 126, 135
Web charts, 19, 158
WomenInk of New York, 54
World Health Organization, 81
Wounded healers, 100–101